THE McNEIL CENTER FOR
EARLY AMERICAN
S T U D I E S

THE AMERICAN REVOLUTION

THE
AMERICAN
REVOLUTION

A Concise History

Robert J. Allison

OXFORD
UNIVERSITY PRESS

OXFORD
UNIVERSITY PRESS

Oxford University Press, Inc., publishes works that further
Oxford University's objective of excellence
in research, scholarship, and education.

Oxford   New York
Auckland   Cape Town   Dar es Salaam   Hong Kong   Karachi
Kuala Lumpur   Madrid   Melbourne   Mexico City   Nairobi
New Delhi   Shanghai   Taipei   Toronto

With offices in
Argentina   Austria   Brazil   Chile   Czech Republic   France   Greece
Guatemala   Hungary   Italy   Japan   Poland   Portugal   Singapore
South Korea   Switzerland   Thailand   Turkey   Ukraine   Vietnam

Copyright © 2011 by Oxford University Press, Inc.

Published by Oxford University Press, Inc.
198 Madison Avenue, New York, NY 10016

www.oup.com

Library of Congress Cataloging-in-Publication Data
Allison, Robert J.
The American Revolution : a concise history / Robert J. Allison.
p.   cm.
Includes bibliographical references and index.
ISBN 978–0–19–531295–9
1. United States—History—Revolution, 1775–1783.   I. Title.
E208.A425 2011
973.3—dc22
2010026412

1 3 5 7 9 8 6 4 2

Printed in the United States of America
on acid-free paper

For Matthew and Susan Galbraith
Ever learning new things

CONTENTS

IMPORTANT DATES IN THE

AMERICAN REVOLUTION

1754
June 19   Albany Conference
July 3   Washington defeated at Fort Necessity

1755
July 9   Braddock defeated in Pennsylvania

1759
September 13   British capture Quebec

1760
September 8   British forces take Montreal

1761   Writs of Assistance case

1763   Treaty of Paris
                           British government bars settlements west
                               of Alleghenies
                           Pontiac's Rebellion

1764   Parliament passes Sugar Act.

1765
March 22   Parliament passes Stamp Act
August 14 & 26   Stamp Act Riots in Boston
October 7–25   Stamp Act Congress meets in New York

1766
March 17   Parliament repeals Stamp Act

1767
June 29   Townshend Acts impose new tariffs on British
                          goods

1768
June 10   John Hancock's ship *Liberty* seized for failure
                          to pay taxes
November 1   British troops arrive in Boston

1770
January 19–20   Sons of Liberty and British soldiers skirmish at
                          Golden Hill, Manhattan
March 5   Boston Massacre
April 12   Parliament repeals all Townshend duties
                          except on tea

1771
May 16   Regulators defeated at Battle of Alamance

1772
June 9   *Gaspee* burned

1773
April 27   Parliament passes Tea Act
December 16   Boston Tea Party

1774
March 31   Parliament closes port of Boston
May 20   King approves suspension of Massachusetts
                          government
June 22   Quebec Act
September 5–   First Continental Congress meets in
    October 16   Philadelphia
September 17   Congress adopts Suffolk Resolves

1775
February 9   King declares Massachusetts to be in rebellion
April 19   Battles of Lexington and Concord

May	Ethan Allen and Benedict Arnold capture Fort Ticonderoga
	Congress reconvenes in Philadelphia
June 17	Battle of Bunker Hill
July 3	Washington takes command of Continental Army
November 7	Lord Dunmore offers liberty to slaves who rebel against rebellious masters

1776

January 1	Lord Dunmore has Norfolk burned
January 10	Thomas Paine publishes *Common Sense*
February 27	Battle of Moore's Creek Bridge
March 17	British evacuate Boston
June 4–28	Clinton fails to take Charleston, South Carolina
July 2	Congress adopts Independence
July 4	Congress adopts Declaration of Independence
August 27	Battle of Long Island
September 11	Peace conference on Staten Island; Franklin, Adams, and Edward Rutledge meet Admiral Howe
September 15	British forces land on Manhattan
September 20–21	New York fire
October 28	Battle of White Plains; American flotilla defeated on Lake Champlain
November 16	British take Fort Washington
November 20	British take Fort Lee
December 26	Battle of Trenton

1777

January 3	Battle of Princeton
July 5	Burgoyne takes Ticonderoga
August 16	Battle of Bennington
September 11	Battle of Brandywine
September 26	British occupy Philadelphia
October 4	Battle of Germantown
October 17	Burgoyne surrenders at Saratoga
Winter 1777–1778	Washington and army at Valley Forge

1778

February 6	France recognizes American independence
April	French fleet sails for America
April 23	John Paul Jones attacks British Isles
June 18	British evacuate Philadelphia
June 28	Battle of Monmouth
August 29	Americans and French fail to take Newport
September 23	*Bonhomme Richard* fights the *Serapis*
December 29	British capture Savannah

1779

February 25	Americans capture Vincennes
June 4	Virginia legislature considers but rejects Statute for Religious Freedom
June 16	Spain declares war on England
October 28	French and American forces end unsuccessful siege of Savannah

1780

March 14	Spanish capture Mobile
May 12	Charleston surrenders to British
July 11	French army and fleet arrive at Newport
August 16	Battle of Camden (South Carolina)
September 23	Discovery of Benedict Arnold's treason
October 7	Battle of King's Mountain
December 20	Britain declares war on Dutch

1781

January 5	Arnold captures Richmond
January 17	Battle of Cowpens
March 15	Battle of Guilford Courthouse
May 9	Spain captures Pensacola
August 4	Cornwallis occupies Yorktown
September 5–9	French defeat British fleet off Chesapeake
October 19	Cornwallis surrenders at Yorktown

1782

November 30	Treaty of Paris signed

1783

March 15	Washington puts down Newburgh conspiracy

June 21	Pennsylvania mutiny
July 8	Massachusetts jury rules that slavery violates state constitution
September 3	Treaty of Paris signed, ending war
October 7	Virginia grants freedom to slaves who served in war
November 25	British evacuate New York
December 23	Washington resigns commission

1784

1785

1786

January 16	Virginia passes Statute for Religious Freedom
August 29	Insurgent Massachusetts farmers put down courts
September 11–14	Annapolis conference proposes revising Articles of Confederation

1787

January 25	Shays's Rebellion put down in Massachusetts
May 25–September 17	Convention drafts new Constitution
July 13	Congress passes Northwest Ordinance
December 7	Delaware ratifies Constitution
December 12	Pennsylvania ratifies Constitution
December 18	New Jersey ratifies Constitution

1788

January 2	Georgia ratifies Constitution
January 9	Connecticut ratifies Constitution
February 6	Massachusetts ratifies Constitution, proposes amendments
April 28	Maryland ratifies Constitution, proposes amendments
May 23	South Carolina ratifies Constitution, proposes amendments
June 21	New Hampshire ratifies Constitution
June 25	Virginia narrowly ratifies Constitution, proposes amendments
June 26	New York ratifies Constitution

June 26   American ships establish trade between Columbia River and China

1789

February 4   George Washington elected president, John Adams vice president

March 4   New U.S. Congress meets in New York

April 30   Washington inaugurated as president

September 25   Congress approves constitutional amendments (Bill of Rights)

November 21   North Carolina, which rejected Constitution in 1788, ratifies

1790

May 29   After rejecting constitution in 1788, Rhode Island ratifies

October   Miami, Shawnee, Delaware defeat U.S. forces at Maumee River

1791

February 25   Washington signs bill creating Bank of the United States

March 3   Congress approves whiskey tax

1791

March 4   Vermont joins union

November 4   Miami confederacy defeat American troops at Wabash River

December 15   Bill of Rights ratified

1792

June 1   Kentucky joins union

1793   Eli Whitney develops cotton gin

April 22   President Washington declares U.S. neutral in war between England and France

1794

March 27   Congress authorizes building of frigates to defend American ships from Barbary states

July–August   Whiskey Rebellion

August 20	United States defeats Miamis and others at Battle of Fallen Timbers
November 19	United States and Britain make treaty
1796	
June 1	Tennessee joins union
September	Washington announces he will not be a candidate for reelection
December 7	John Adams elected president, Thomas Jefferson vice president
1797	
October 18	French officials demand bribes from American diplomats
1797–1800	War with France
1798	First American trading voyage to Japan
	American ships reach Arabia
July 14	Congress passes Sedition Act
1799	
December 14	George Washington dies
1801	Thomas Jefferson elected President
1801–1805	War with Tripoli
1803	United States purchases Louisiana Territory from France
1807	
June 22	British warship *Leopard* attacks USS *Chesapeake* off Virginia coast
1808	
January 1	United States bans the trans-Atlantic slave trade
	Embargo closes American ports
1811	
November 7	U.S. forces defeat Shawnee at Tippecanoe

1812

June 18	United States declares war on Great Britain
August 16	Detroit surrenders to British and Native American forces
August 19	USS *Constitution* defeats HMS *Guerrierre*

1813

October 5	Battle of Thames, Shawnee warrior Tecumseh killed

1814

March 27	American, Cherokee, and Choctaw warriors defeat Creeks at Horseshoe Bend, Alabama
December 24	American and British negotiators agree on peace treaty at Ghent, Belgium

1815

January 8	Battle of New Orleans

1824

August 15	Lafayette arrives as guest of nation

1825

June 16	Cornerstone of Bunker Hill Monument laid

1826

July 4	Thomas Jefferson and John Adams die

"The History of our Revolution will be one continued lye from one end to the other," John Adams predicted. "The essence of the whole will be *that Dr. Franklin's electrical Rod smote the Earth and out sprung General Washington. That Franklin electrified him with his rod—and thence forward these two conducted all the Policy, Negotiations, Legislatures, and War.*"

Adams objected partly because this fanciful retelling ignored him. But it also ignored other details, such as causes and consequences. What caused the Revolution? Political oppression? Economic hardship? Parliament reduced taxes on Americans, who were growing more prosperous than the English; despite widespread rioting in the colonies, the only people the British government arrested in the 1760s and 1770s were British soldiers who shot at protesting Americans.

The American protests over taxes and government produced a new kind of political system in which the majority governs, but individuals maintain their liberty.

The story of individuals protecting their rights in a system where the majority governs begins in the Revolution, when men and women set out to protect their liberty by mobilizing their neighbors and public opinion. To understand how this system came into being, if it was not simply created by Franklin's lightning rod and an electrified Washington, we must look into the "Policy, Negotiations, Legislatures, and War," and the many people who brought the Revolution about.

ACKNOWLEDGMENTS

As this book introduces the American Revolution, I thank those who introduced me to that event. My mother, who hates history, took me to Washington's headquarters in Morristown; through a window I caught a quick glimpse of a white wig and a Continental uniform as a mysterious figure rose from Washington's desk, then vanished. Ever since I have trailed that elusive phantom, and thank many good park rangers—in New Jersey, Massachusetts, and points south and west—for bringing us closer.

My late friend Mike Bare brought Fort Ticonderoga together with South Boston, Roxbury, and Dorchester; his memory will be cherished with the events he nobly reimagined. I am indebted to him and to the noble reimaginings of Bernard Bailyn, Robert Bellinger, John Cavanagh, David Hackett Fischer, William Fowler, Robert Gross, Robert Hall, Susan Lively, Pauline Maier, Louis Masur, Joseph McCarthy, Drew McCoy, Joseph McEttrick (thanks to whom I was both juror and defendant in the Boston Massacre Trial), Gary Nash, John Tyler, Ted Widmer, and Matt Wilding.

The Boston National Historical Park, Bostonian Society, Old South Meeting House, Adams National Historic Site, Grand Lodge of Free and Accepted Masons of Philadelphia, Massachusetts State Archives, Paul Revere House, Shirley-Eustis House, Salem Athenaeum, Exploritas, and teacher workshops (under the Teaching American History program, Primary Source, and Outward Bound/Expeditionary Learning) in Massachusetts, Illinois, and Tennessee, allowed me to share this story with engaged audiences, whose questions and challenges helped me think it through. Students of the American Revolution, Benjamin Franklin, and Boston history at Suffolk University and the Harvard Extension School have enriched my understanding with their questions, comments, and their own research.

At the Massachusetts Historical Society, I thank Peter Drummey, Anne Bentley, and Elaine Grublin for all their assistance, and, at the Massachusetts State Archives, special thanks to Michael Comeau. Deans Kenneth S. Greenberg at Suffolk and Michael Shinagel at the Harvard Extension School have with consistent enthusiasm supported scholarship and teaching.

Susan Ferber at Oxford University Press patiently coaxed this book along; each page bears evidence of her good sense and clear eye. The greatest thanks go to my wife, Phyllis, and sons, John Robert and Philip. May the story engage them as I still am by the flash of white wig and red and blue coat glimpsed long ago through a Morristown window.

Robert J. Allison
Boston, Massachusetts
Bunker Hill Day, 2010

THE AMERICAN REVOLUTION

CHAPTER I

THE REVOLUTION'S ORIGINS

To a British policy maker in the 1750s, the "colonies" were Barbados or Jamaica, the important sugar-producing islands in the West Indies, or the rich provinces of India, whose governments and finances the East India Company was taking over. If he turned his attention to North America, his focus would not be on Massachusetts, Virginia, or Pennsylvania, but on the vast interior beyond the mountains, the area drained by the Ohio and Mississippi Rivers. The Crown claimed this territory under grants it had given to the separate colonies, though the Iroquois, Miami, Shawnee, Cherokee, and other native people possessed it. But in the 1750s the French were moving in from Canada and Louisiana, coming down the Great Lakes and up the Mississippi to trade furs and make treaties with the native people, and building forts at Detroit, Vincennes (now in Indiana), and St. Louis. From Quebec to New Orleans, the French were taking control of the continent's interior. British policy makers paid little attention to their Atlantic outposts, but they could not ignore the interior. Having gained India, the British were about to lose North America.

The Atlantic colonies had grown despite British policy. Although not as lucrative as England's sugar colonies, they were essential to the sugar economy. Religious dissenters had planted the New England colonies— Massachusetts, New Hampshire, Rhode Island, and Connecticut—in the seventeenth century. By the mid-eighteenth century, they were prospering through trade. New England's forests were turned into ships and barrels to carry the British Empire's goods, and cod caught off New England's coast fed the slave laborers of the West Indies. Boston and Newport had become busy ports. The culturally homogeneous New Englanders had rebuffed a 1688 attempt by England to restructure their government; the people of New England had more power to govern themselves than anyone else in the British Empire, power they jealously guarded.

The British had taken New York from the Dutch in 1664 but preserved the colony's commercial system: trade with the Iroquois, the most powerful Native Americans in North America, and rule by a landholding elite. New York City, on the southern tip of Manhattan Island, and Albany, up the Hudson River, were the most important trading centers, but New York's hegemony stretched into New Jersey, whose farmland fed the Manhattan settlement as well as the towns of New Brunswick and Elizabeth. New York also claimed Long Island and the coast of Connecticut, and all the up-river territory between the Hudson, Lake Champlain, and the Connecticut River. New Englanders did not recognize New York's imperial dreams.

Pennsylvania, which culturally included the three counties of Delaware, as well as the areas of New Jersey on the Delaware River's east bank, had been founded by Quakers in the 1680s. Determined to be fair to the native people, Pennsylvania's merchants defied New York's claim to a monopoly on trade with the Iroquois by trading with the Tuscarora and Lenape, whom the Iroquois considered their own dependents. Richer soil and a milder climate made Pennsylvania better farmland than New England; fairer land distribution made it more appealing than New York or the colonies further south. By 1750 Philadelphia was the empire's second busiest port, sending grain to feed the laborers in Barbados and Jamaica, and bringing in English, German, and Scotch-Irish immigrants to become independent farmers.

The Chesapeake colonies of Virginia and Maryland, founded early in the seventeenth century, were by the middle of the eighteenth home to mature plantation societies. Large farms used slave labor to grow tobacco for the world market. In area and population, Virginia—with half a million people—was the largest mainland colony; one of every six Americans lived in Virginia, and two of every five Virginians were slaves. Tobacco cultivation had exhausted the tidewater soil; tobacco planters were looking inland, beyond the mountains, for more land for planting and selling.

North Carolina's coastal towns—New Bern and Edenton—were trading centers for tobacco gentry, much like the Chesapeake ports. But the interior was rapidly being settled by Scotch-Irish and German immigrants, making their way down the piedmont from Pennsylvania, more than quadrupling North Carolina's population by 1770, and making it the fourth-largest and fastest-growing mainland colony. The settlers on the backcountry borders with the Cherokee and Catawba were farmers, not planters; they did not recognize the coastal planters' cultural or political superiority.

Immigrants were also filling South Carolina's backcountry, making it a different society than the coastal low country, which Barbadian and Jamaican planters with their slaves and rice plantations had settled in the 1680s. 60 percent of South Carolina's people were enslaved people of color; on some coastal rice plantations, 90 percent of the people were slaves. Slave labor made South Carolina possible, and slaves built Charlestown (renamed Charleston in 1783), the only urban center south of Philadelphia. The white minority held on to power, having survived a slave revolt in 1739, but planters were wary of the growing power of the backcountry.

Georgia was the newest and smallest colony, with barely thirty thousand people, half of them enslaved. Founded in the 1730s as a barrier between South Carolina and Spanish Florida, Georgia gave British traders entrée into trade with the Creek and Cherokee, and a wedge against Spanish and French traders of Pensacola and New Orleans. It also was to be a refuge for England's debtors and poor. The debtors and poor arrived in Georgia and wondered why they could not own slaves, as the whites across the Savannah River in South Carolina did. Their philanthropic sponsors eventually relented to the white Georgians' demand for slaves, so Georgia shared the slave labor economy of South Carolina. Spanish Florida marked frontier to the south, as did the Creek and Cherokee lands to the west.

Thirteen colonies, with very different populations, economic systems, social structures, and with no formal communication system joining them except through London. Post roads linked Boston with Philadelphia, but most transit was by water, and few Americans had visited the other colonies. George Washington visited Barbados as a youth, but not Philadelphia or New York; John Adams, of Massachusetts, did not see New York or Philadelphia until he was nearly forty.

Problems of communication and transportation had not stopped the colonies' growth. Benjamin Franklin, an American who had traveled, reflected that though only eighty thousand English people had come to America since 1607, by 1751 more than a million English descendants lived in America, along with growing numbers of Germans, Africans, and

Scotch-Irish. England's population had risen from five to six million between 1700 and 1750; in that same time America's population doubled. Franklin predicted it would double again in twenty-five years, and by 1850 the "greatest Number of *Englishmen* will be on this Side the Water. What an Accession of Power to the *British* Empire by Sea as well as Land! What Increase of Trade and Navigation! What numbers of Ships and Seamen!"

Franklin anticipated that these colonies would remain part of a thriving British empire. But there was an immediate threat. The French were taking control of the interior from the Saint Lawrence to the Mississippi, which threatened British control of the continent.

Virginians had built a small fort where the Alleghany and Monongahela Rivers joined to form the Ohio, garrisoning it with forty-four men to trade with the Delaware, Shawnee, Seneca, and Mingo. In April 1754, a force of French and Indians—the garrison thought there were a thousand of them—came down from Lake Erie on a fleet of 360 bateaux with heavy artillery. The Virginians surrendered, giving up £20,000 worth of trade goods.

The British colonies would not unite against this threat. New York and Pennsylvania each wanted its own merchants to control the Indian trade; Virginia planters speculated in Indian hunting grounds along the Ohio; Massachusetts and New York were on the verge of war over the land between the Connecticut and Hudson rivers; Connecticut and Pennsylvania both claimed the lands of the Lenape on the upper Susquehanna, or Wyoming, valley; Georgia and South Carolina competed for trade with the Creek and Cherokee. Survival depended on cooperation, but this would require each colony to overlook its immediate self-interest.

Alarmed at French encroachments, the British government ordered the colonies to meet with the Iroquois leaders to secure their alliance against the French. In the summer of 1754 delegates from seven colonies assembled at Albany, New York. The conference was a failure. Individual colonial agents made separate peaces with the Iroquois (Virginia bought Kentucky lands from the Iroquois, though the lands were Shawnee) but devised no united strategy. The conference approved a plan of union, drawn up by Franklin and the Massachusetts politician Thomas Hutchinson, under which each colony would choose delegates to a forty-eight-member grand council, which would meet every year in a different colonial capital; this council would raise troops and taxes from the colonies for common defense, though each colony would continue to govern itself. The king would appoint a president-general, to ensure that the council did not conflict with British policy.

Though the Albany conference approved the plan, the colonial assemblies would not. None would cede any of its powers or prerogatives to the other colonies. Somewhat bitterly, Franklin said the colonies would only unite if the British government forced them to do so.

Meanwhile, Virginia sent Lieutenant Colonel George Washington and provincial troops to the Alleghany and Monongahela; in a muddled skirmish, a French diplomat was killed. The French counterattacked, captured the fort Washington had built (Fort Necessity) and sent Washington back to Virginia. These frontier skirmishes led England and France to declare war on each other. This war that Washington started on the Monongahela spread from North America to the Caribbean, to Africa and Europe and the Mediterranean, to India and the Pacific. It was the first global war. Prime minister William Pitt recognized that the keys to victory were control of the seas and of North America. Pitt mobilized British ships and regulars and thousands of American militia troops to wrest Montreal and Quebec from the French. A subsequent force took Cuba and Florida from Spain. At the war's end Britain claimed all of America east of the Mississippi.

The British had the Ohio territory, but had not reckoned with the native people in it. Ottawa leader Pontiac led an uprising of the Native Americans against the British, quickly overwhelming their small garrisons and taking every British outpost except Fort Pitt. Could Britain send enough troops to protect settlers in this vast territory?

The British saw that more white settlement in the area—which Pontiac effectively blocked—would have more conflicts with Native Americans, which would require more troops. To avoid these problems, and put a stop to the squabbles between New York, Pennsylvania, and Virginia, the British crown simply barred white settlement and sale of lands between the Appalachian Mountains and the Mississippi, from Quebec to Florida. Every colony from Georgia to Connecticut resented this Proclamation of 1763. Why had they gone to war if they were to be kept out of Ohio?

Reaction against the proclamation, though, was mild compared to the reaction against Parliament's attempts to regulate colonial trade and to pay for the defense of the colonial frontiers. Parliament began its fiscal campaign with the Sugar Act in April 1764. This cut the tax on imported molasses in half, to three pence per gallon, but, unlike the previous tax, this one contained provisions to ensure collection. Merchants would have to post a bond, guaranteeing their obedience, and violators would be tried not by juries, but by judges in specially created vice-admiralty courts.

Along with passing the Sugar Act, Parliament prohibited colonies from coining or printing their own money. The object was to standardize currency and prevent wildly fluctuating notes and coins, but the real effect was to take money out of circulation and stifle colonial trade.

Predictably, merchants protested. Less predictable was their rationale for protesting: they contended that they could not be taxed without their own consent; they had not elected Parliament, and so it could not tax them. And if Parliament could tax them, it could control them in other ways. Boston lawyer James Otis wrote in 1764 that it was not the tax but the principle that was wrong. If the colonists could be taxed without their consent, they were in fact slaves of Parliament:

> The colonists, being men, have a right to be considered as equally entitled to all the rights of nature with the Europeans, and they are not to be restrained in the exercise of any of these rights but for the evident good of the whole community. By being or becoming members of society they have not renounced their natural liberty in any greater degree than other good citizens, and if 'tis taken from them without their consent they are so far enslaved.

He went on to argue that slavery was wrong for whites as well as blacks:

> The colonists are by the law of nature freeborn, as indeed all men are, white or black.... Does it follow that 'tis right to enslave a man because he is black? Will short curled hair like wool instead of Christian hair, as 'tis called by those whose hearts are as hard as the nether millstone, help the argument? Can any logical inference in favor of slavery be drawn from a flat nose, a long or a short face?...It is a clear truth that those who every day barter away other men's liberty will soon care little for their own.

Otis continued: "Are not women born as free as men? Would it not be infamous to assert that the ladies are all slaves by nature?" In arguing against Parliament's power to tax the sugar trade, Otis advanced arguments against any kind of arbitrary power. Otis saw the end result of the sugar tax as enslavement; he also saw the end of his opposition as liberating men and women, black and white, to enjoy the fruits of their own labor.

Parliament moved quickly down the path Otis predicted. Lord George Grenville, the British chancellor of the exchequer, proposed a stamp tax for the American colonies, taxing all printed documents—newspapers, pamphlets, college diplomas, deeds, bills of sale and bills of lading, marriage licenses, legal documents, playing cards, dice, wills—at rates from three pence to four pounds each, depending on the document's value, payable in hard currency. Proof of payment would be in the form of a stamp affixed to the document. In support of the tax, Charles Townshend in February 1765 asked if "these Americans, Children planted by our Care, nourished up by our Indulgence until they are grown to a Degree of Strength & Opulence, and protected by our Arms," would "grudge to contribute their mite to relieve us from the heavy weight of that burden which we lie under?"

Immediately Isaac Barre disputed Townshend's interpretation of colonial history. "They planted by your Care? No! your Oppressions planted em in America.... They nourished up by *your* indulgence? they grew by your neglect of Em... They protected by *your* Arms? they have nobly taken up Arms in your defence." He said the Americans were "as truly Loyal as any Subjects the King has, but a people Jealous of their Lyberties and who will vindicate them," especially against officials and policies that "caused the Blood of those Sons of Liberty to recoil within them."

American opponents of the Stamp Act, which Parliament passed on March 22, 1765, began calling themselves Sons of Liberty. They built on other institutions, particularly the colonial press: Benjamin Edes of Boston, printer of the *Boston Gazette*, William Goddard of the *Providence Gazette*, Samuel Hall of the *Newport Mercury*, and William Bradford of the *Pennsylvania Journal* were all critical leaders of the Sons of Liberty, whose real strength came from each community's working people. For example, Ebenezer MacIntosh, a Boston shoemaker, longtime leader of Boston's South End Mob, became the "captain general of the Sons of Liberty," and the large elm from which his mob had hung effigies of unpopular officials became the "Liberty Tree."

Patrick Henry in the Virginia assembly (the House of Burgesses) in May 1765 proposed resolutions that "the distinguishing characteristick of British freedom" is the right to be taxed only by one's own consent, and the people of Virginia had not given up this right. Though the assembly rejected Henry's resolutions, the press published them throughout the colonies, making them the basis for each colony's opposition.

In Boston rumors circulated that Andrew Oliver, a merchant, secretary to the provincial government, brother-in-law of Lieutenant Governor Thomas Hutchinson, and newly appointed tax agent, was storing the revenue stamps in his waterfront warehouse. A mob tore the warehouse apart on the night of August 14, 1765 and tossed the debris into the harbor. There were no stamps inside. Two weeks later a mob ransacked Lieutenant Governor Hutchinson's house, driving out Hutchinson and his daughter and destroying everything within. Stamp agents in every colony but Georgia resigned.

James Otis called for all colonies to send delegates to a congress in New York in October to draw up a common protest against the Stamp Act. Nine colonies (all but Virginia, New Hampshire, North Carolina, and Georgia) sent delegates, who drew up a careful protest against the act, saying they had "the warmest sentiments of affection and duty to His Majesty's person and government" but that the stamp tax not only imposed a burden on them, it violated their rights as British subjects. They sent their petition to King George III, who received it but referred the matter to Parliament.

As the petition made its way to London, the Stamp Act went into effect on November 1. Ebenezer MacIntosh organized protest parades in Boston and that night walked through the streets arm in arm with merchant William Brattle, a member of the Governor's Council, showing unity between Boston's commercial leaders and emerging political leaders like MacIntosh, whose power came from an ability to mobilize dockworkers, longshoremen, and rope makers to attack the Oliver warehouse or hang effigies from the Liberty Tree. Resistance now could afford to be more civil. Americans showed a near-unanimous determination to boycott the stamps, and word reached the colonies that Grenville's government had fallen. Massachusetts Lieutenant Governor Hutchinson reported in March 1766 that "the authority of every colony is in the hands of the sons of liberty," and customs agent John Robinson reported that stamp officers felt the anger "not of a trifling Mob, but of a whole Country."

Parliament wanted to know why Americans had united in opposition, so it summoned the Pennsylvania Assembly's London lobbyist, Benjamin Franklin, to explain. Franklin told them their insistence on taxing Americans had changed Americans' opinion of Parliament. No longer was it "the great bulwark and security of their liberties and privileges." Unless Parliament repealed the Stamp Act, Americans would lose their

Die Americaner wiedersetzen sich der Stempel Acte, und verbrennen das aus England nach America gesandte Stempel Papier zu Boston. im August 1764.

Mobs took to the streets in protest of the Stamp Act of 1765. (Image courtesy of the Massachusetts Historical Society.)

"respect and affection" for the British and, more important, cut off "all the commerce that depends on that respect and affection." Once proud to "indulge in the fashions and manufactures of Great Britain," Americans now proudly wore "their old clothes over again, till they can make new ones." They had given up their custom of wearing black mourning accessories rather than buy them from the British, and they gave up eating lamb so that the lambs could grow into wool-producing sheep. Franklin told Parliament that "the sweet little creatures are all alive to this day, with the prettiest fleeces on their backs imaginable."

If Parliament repealed the Stamp Act, would the colonies give up their claim that Parliament could not tax them?

"No, never," Franklin said. "They will never do it, unless compelled by force of arms," but "No power, how great soever, can force men to change their opinions."

Could anything other than military power enforce the Stamp Act?

Not even an army could enforce the stamp law in America. Soldiers would "find nobody in arms" there. "They will not find a rebellion; they may indeed make one."

Former prime minister William Pitt called on Parliament to repeal the "unhappy," "unconstitutional," "unjust," and "oppressive" act, and asked how Parliament could justify not giving three million Americans representation, when an English "borough with half a Dozen houses" had a representative. Pitt predicted that this "rotten Part of our Constitution" would not survive, warning that the struggle with America would force England to reform her own government.

Parliament rescinded the Stamp Act but passed the Declaratory Act, which asserted its power to control the colonies "in all cases whatsoever."

Americans greeted the repeal as a victory within, not over, the British Empire. Philadelphians held off celebrating until June 4, when they observed George III's birthday. John Adams wrote that the "people are as quiet and submissive to Government as any people under the sun; as little inclined to tumults, riots, seditions, as they were ever known to be since the first foundation of the Government." He said the repeal "has composed every wave of popular discord into a smooth and peaceful calm." This was a great change from the tumults, riots, and seditions of 1765. Americans believed those protests, petitions, and warnings about loss of trade, had forced Parliament to rescind the law. They could live with the Declaratory Act as long as Parliament did not enforce it.

But in 1767 Charles Townshend, chancellor of the exchequer, proposed a new series of revenue laws, taxing all lead, glass, paint, and tea imported into the colonies. Customs collectors were sent to America to make sure the taxes were paid, and new courts of admiralty were created to hear cases of ships violating the revenue acts. These new revenue laws, known as the Townshend Acts, touched off renewed political and social agitation.

Philadelphia lawyer John Dickinson wrote a series of essays, *Farmer's Letters*, arguing that Parliament did not have the power to tax the colonies. Dickinson conceded that Parliament could regulate commerce, but he insisted that the colonists could only be taxed by their own consent, by assemblies they had chosen.

When New York's assembly protested that Parliament did not have the power to raise revenues in the colonies, the governor, Sir Henry Moore, suspended the assembly. Governor Francis Bernard demanded that the Massachusetts Assembly rescind the letter it sent to other colonies urging resistance; when the assembly refused, Bernard dissolved it. These attacks on assemblies transformed the struggle into one between arbitrary executive power and government by the people. Leaders of the suspended assemblies and the Sons of Liberty organized boycotts of British goods.

Women took to their spinning wheels—what had been a chore for solitary women, spinning wool into yarn, weaving yarn into cloth, now became a public political act. Ninety-two "Daughters of Liberty" brought their wheels to the meeting house in Newport, spending the day spinning together until they produced 170 skeins of yarn. Making and wearing homespun cloth became political acts of resistance.

Fearing the boycotts and resistance would turn violent, Governor Bernard asked for British troops to keep peace in Boston. Two British regiments arrived in October 1768. Benjamin Franklin thought that sending troops to Boston would be "like setting up a smith's forge in a magazine of gunpowder."

Franklin was proven right. On March 5, 1770, rioters attacked the main British barracks, and in the ensuing street fight soldiers fired on a crowd of civilians. Five civilians were killed in what town leaders quickly called the "Horrid Massacre." Paul Revere made an engraving of the scene, showing an orderly line of troops shooting at innocent and unarmed civilians, with the state house and the First Church looming over the tragedy; in this depiction the arbitrary power of the soldiers has usurped Boston's legitimate civil and spiritual authority.

In the wake of the violence, Boston's town government demanded removal of the troops, warning that ten thousand people in surrounding communities were ready to march in and drive the soldiers out. Lieutenant Governor Thomas Hutchinson (acting as governor after Bernard's return to England) complied, having the soldiers involved in the shooting arrested and the others sent to New Jersey.

Two leading patriots, as the opponents of the tax laws called themselves, stepped forward to defend the accused soldiers. Josiah Quincy and John Adams wanted the troops out of town, but they also wanted to prove that Boston was not the ungovernable and riotous place Bernard

Paul Revere's engraving shaped the way Americans thought of the Massacre: British soldiers stand in a straight line firing into an unarmed crowd. A gun fires from the window of the Custom House (labeled "Butcher's Hall"). Looming above are the state house and First Church—legitimate government and spiritual order usurped by the armed men in uniform. (Image courtesy of the Massachusetts State Archives.)

had described. By giving British soldiers who shot unarmed civilians in the streets of Boston a fair trial, Quincy and Adams could prove that the people of Boston were law abiding. Two soldiers were found guilty of manslaughter, still a capital offense. Adams had their sentence reduced to branding on the thumbs, and the rest were acquitted. With the troops gone, Boston calmed down. Parliament eased the tension by repealing most of the Townshend duties, but to prove that it still could tax the Americans, it left in place the tax on tea.

The colonies agreed on little other than that Parliament could not tax them. Massachusetts and New York had a long-standing dispute over the land between the Connecticut and Hudson rivers, and New York was on the verge of war with New Hampshire over Vermont, with the people of that area adamantly against being part of either. Pennsylvania and Connecticut both claimed the Wyoming Valley, which Connecticut settlers were farming under their seventeenth-century charter.

American hunger for land led to conflict among the colonial governments and with the native people; from Massachusetts to Georgia, white settlers eyed the land of the native people. The Mashpee Wampanoag of Cape Cod sent a delegation to ask the king to protect them from the Massachusetts government, which allowed whites to buy their land. In the Carolinas and Georgia, farmers in the backcountry were moving into the lands of the Cherokee and Creek. North Carolina sent Daniel Boone west to buy the land between the Tennessee and Cumberland rivers from the Cherokee, despite the fact that the Cherokee did not own it.

Virginia's royal governor, Lord Dunmore, wrote to Lord Dartmouth, the secretary of state for American affairs, that the Proclamation of 1763 that closed off the trans-Appalachian west was "insufficient to restrain the Americans, and that they do and will remove as their avidity and restlessness incite them." The Americans had "no attachment to Place, but wandering about seems engrafted in their Nature," Dunmore said, but they "imagine the lands further off, are Still better than those upon which they are already settled."

Dunmore saw two possible outcomes. Settlers might move into the territories and intermarry with the Indians, "the dreadful consequences" of which "may be easily foreseen." Or the provincial governments could supervise the westward movement, allowing white settlers "to form a Set of Democratical Governments of their own, upon the backs of the Old Colonies." Dunmore found neither option palatable, but decided the Virginia government should take control of the frontier.

Under Dunmore's orders, Dr. John Connolly rebuilt the abandoned Fort Pitt in 1774, renamed it Fort Dunmore, and from it started a war against the Shawnees and Mingos of Kentucky and Ohio. Sir William Johnson kept the Iroquois from supporting their Mingo and Shawnee allies against Virginia. Without Iroquois support, the Shawnee and Mingo could not hold off the aggressive Virginians, who won hunting rights in Kentucky and what is now West Virginia.

North Carolina had just emerged from its own civil war. Farmers in the piedmont were outraged that the government, based on the seacoast, controlled their land and taxed them. Government agents—magistrates and justices of the peace—charged excessive fees. Fearing riots by the piedmont farmers, and knowing that juries would stand by their neighbors, North Carolina's government ordered that trials for frontier troublemakers be held at New Bern, where Governor Thomas Tryon was building, at taxpayer's expense, an elegant governor's palace. Outraged at a government that taxed but did not protect or represent them, North Carolina's backcountry farmers set out to regulate their own affairs, shutting down the courts and taking the law into their own hands. Tryon raised troops to suppress the "Regulators," defeating them in a pitched battle at Alamance Creek in 1771. Suppressed but not defeated, the Regulators of North Carolina continued to be deeply suspicious of distant and unresponsive governments. Tryon left North Carolina to become governor of New York.

All was still relatively quiet in Massachusetts. "If it were not for an Adams or two," newly appointed governor Thomas Hutchinson wrote, "we should do well enough." Samuel Adams was not idle. Following the model of the Sons of Liberty, who had established a communication network among like-minded people in the different colonies, Adams in November 1772 created the Boston Committee of Correspondence, a twenty-one-member group to keep in contact with like-minded people in other towns. "We are brewing something here which will make some people's heads reel...," Dr. Thomas Young wrote. As Massachusetts towns formed Committees of Correspondence, Adams, as clerk of the Massachusetts Assembly, had that body form a Committee of Correspondence to communicate with other assemblies. By 1774, every colonial assembly had a committee to correspond with the other assemblies; this ensured that Boston would not be isolated during the crisis that quickly ensued.

"The seditious here have raised a flame in every colony," General Gage wrote home to England. He blamed the English opposition's "speeches, writings, and protests" for fanning the flames of colonial discontent. London gossip Horace Walpole called this a cruel charge against the Americans, that the weak and disorganized British opposition stirred their dissent: "Might as soon light a fire with a wet dishclout."

Americans did not need the British opposition, as the government itself effectively lit the fire. Admiral John Montagu's fleet patrolled the American coast, ostensibly for smugglers. Lieutenant William Dudingston on the *Gaspee* was certain every fishing boat and merchant vessel he saw off Rhode Island was smuggling. He stopped and searched every vessel he could, and reprovisioned the *Gaspee* by raiding Rhode Island farms. When the fishermen and farmers complained to their governor, who in turn complained to the admiral, Montagu warned that he would hang anyone who interfered with Lieutenant Dudingston, who became even more severe in his dealings with Rhode Islanders.

Fishermen and merchants took matters into their own hands. When Dudingston brought the *Gaspee* too close to the Narragansett shore, they boarded, forced the sailors off, and set the schooner on fire. Montagu turned to legal remedies, and from London came the order to seize the culprits and bring them to London for trial as pirates. But Rhode Island chief justice Stephen Hopkins refused to allow their arrest. Admiral Montagu bemoaned the fact that the laws of Parliament would not be enforced in America except by military force.

The British government had not regarded these thirteen colonies, with their different social structures and political systems, as essential parts of the empire as a whole. When the French threatened, the colonists had not united in the interest of the British Empire. But now, as the British government tried to make them cohesive parts of the imperial fabric, the colonists began to unite against the empire that sought to govern them.

CHAPTER 2

REBELLION IN THE COLONIES

GEORGE III WAS THOROUGHLY ENGLISH, AND DETERMINED TO be a "patriot king" in the best Enlightenment tradition. His grandfather, George II, and great-grandfather, George I, were German princes from Hanover; they spoke little or no English and returned regularly to their Germanic principality. But George III never left England and would grace its throne for nearly sixty years. The first decade of his reign was unsteady, until he appointed Frederick, Lord North to be prime minister. Lord North would serve from 1770 until 1782, sharing the king's outlook on the good of the empire.

Neither the king nor his minister was thinking specifically of Americans when North proposed the Tea Act. The measure instead had much to do with the empire and the North ministry. The East India Company had taken over the administration of India; this gave it great potential wealth, as well as immediate and tremendous debt. North proposed lending the Company £1.5 million (about $270 million today). In return, he would appoint the company's governors. The company would also have a monopoly on tea sold in North America, and could ship its tea directly to the American markets without paying British revenue duties.

The "Day is at length arrived," a committee of Philadelphia merchants declared, "in which we must determine to live as Freemen—or as Slaves to linger out a miserable existence." The Tea Act would make Americans subservient to the "corrupt and designing Ministry" and change their "invaluable Title of American Freemen to that of Slaves." Americans must not give Parliament the power to control their lives, they said. The Philadelphians insisted that no tea be landed.

A Boston mob attacked the home of tea merchant Richard Clarke, and when the first tea ship, the *Dartmouth*, reached Boston on November 28, 1773, more than a thousand people crowded into Faneuil Hall to protest its arrival. The Sons of Liberty sent guards to make sure no tea was unloaded. Under British law, a ship could remain in port twenty days without unloading; after that its cargo must be taxed. The Sons of Liberty and the town leaders—Samuel Adams, Josiah Quincy, and others—were determined not to let the tea be unloaded or taxed. The tea merchants— all Americans—wanted the tea unloaded and sold. The ship owners—all Americans—simply wanted their vessels unharmed so they could carry cargo back to England. Two more vessels reached Boston in the ensuing weeks, but none of the other ships had reached the American ports when Bostonians took action on December 16, the night the tea had to be unloaded and the tax paid. That night, Bostonians disguised as Indians boarded the three ships, hoisted the 342 chests up to the decks, and dumped 92,586 pounds of tea, worth £9,659 (about $1.7 million today) into the harbor.

"This is the most magnificent Movement of all," John Adams wrote. "There is a Dignity, a Majesty, a Sublimity, in this last Effort of the Patriots, that I greatly admire. The People should never rise, without doing something to be remembered—something notable And striking. This Destruction of the Tea is so bold, so daring, so firm, intrepid and inflexible, and it must have so important consequences, and so lasting, that I cant but consider it an Epocha in History."

The destruction of the tea (it would not be called the "Boston Tea Party" for fifty years) had dramatic consequences. Paul Revere carried the news to New York, which resolved not to land the tea, and the tea consignees resigned their commissions to sell tea. The news reached Philadelphia the day before Christmas; on Christmas Day the ship *Polly* entered the Delaware. Eight thousand Philadelphians gathered in front of the state house to demand the *Polly* immediately return to England. It did. Americans would not receive the tea. When an errant tea ship sailed into the Chesapeake in April, its owner feared the consequences to himself and his reputation if he were known as a tea merchant. He had the fully loaded ship set on fire.

As Americans united against Parliament and the East India tea, Parliament struck back, closing Boston harbor until the lawless town paid for the tea; suspending Massachusetts's government, and requiring the governor's permission for town meetings; and giving the governor, not the people, the power to choose sheriffs, magistrates, and the Governor's Council. General Thomas Gage, commander of British military forces in North America, was named the new governor, and he was allowed to lodge troops in private homes. Finally, Parliament extended Quebec's boundaries to the Ohio and Mississippi Rivers, cutting that territory off from Virginia, Pennsylvania, and New York and giving Canada's Catholics freedom to practice their religion. North and the British government believed that Massachusetts was particularly rebellious but that most colonists were loyal. Isolate Massachusetts, prevent the rebellious contagion from spreading, and ultimately even the troublesome and factious people of Massachusetts would come to their senses.

New Englanders mobilized to prevent isolation. Rhode Island's assembly called for all colonies to send delegates to a Continental Congress. John Adams predicted that "the wisest Men upon the Continent" would resolve the crisis.

Men and women were engaged now in the cause. Fifty-one women in Edenton, North Carolina, signed a pledge not to buy tea or other British goods. Writing to his family in North Carolina from London, Arthur Iredell asked, "Is there a Female Congress at Edenton, too? I hope not, for we Englishmen are afraid of the Male Congress, but if the Ladies, who have ever, since the Amazonian Era, been esteemed the most formidable enemies, if they, I say, should attack us, the most fatal consequences is to be dreaded." While Iredell's tone was somewhat mocking, the fact that women now were engaged in this political campaign—that British policy had stirred resistance in the homes as well as the taverns and coffee houses—rightly alarmed the policy makers.

Men from every colony except Georgia were represented when Congress gathered in Philadelphia in September 1774. Would the colonies side with Boston? Or would they advise the Bostonians to pay for the tea and to stop being so troublesome?

Outside of Boston, which was now occupied by General Gage and British troops, delegates from Suffolk County's towns met and resolved that the "Intolerable Acts"—shutting the port, suspending the government, extending Quebec, allowing quartering of troops—violated the British constitution. They called for suspending trade with Britain, and, since Parliament had illegally suspended their charter, they called for the people of Massachusetts to form a new government. Paul Revere left Boston with these resolutions on September 11; six days later Congress unanimously endorsed them. Adams called it "one of the happiest Days of my Life," writing in his diary, "This Day convinces me that America will support the Massachusetts or perish with her."

Congress resolved to petition the king to relieve Boston and change policy, and called on the people of Quebec to join them. It proposed meeting again in May 1775 if the British government did not respond favorably to their petition.

In Boston, General Gage tried to defuse the situation. Hearing that the towns were taking gunpowder from a provincial powder house in Cambridge (now in Somerville), Gage had the remaining powder brought to Boston. This provoked wild rumors that the British fleet had bombarded Boston, killing six men. Four thousand men gathered on Cambridge Common. Unable or unwilling to attack Gage or his troops, they stormed the homes of local Tories, who fled to Gage's protection in Boston.

Despite having the king's commission, Gage realized his actual power extended only as far as his troops controlled. The people in the Massachusetts towns recognized a different government—town governments, chosen by majority votes in town meetings. Men and women who wished to remain loyal to the king and the legitimate government had to flee from their homes to be under Gage's protection.

The Portsmouth, New Hampshire, militia surprised and overwhelmed the six British soldiers garrisoning Fort William and Mary in December, spiriting away its cannon and munitions. Salem's militia mobilized in February 1775 to seize cannon from the British regulars. The Americans would not attack the soldiers—they blocked the roads in Salem to stymie the British regulars—but forced them either to surrender or to fire the first shot. "Put your enemy in the wrong, and keep him so," Samuel Adams wrote in March, "is a wise maxim in politics, as well as in war."

Gage and London both failed at conciliation. William Pitt, the former prime minister, proposed pulling Gage's forces from Boston and limiting Parliament's power to tax the colonies. Instead, Parliament followed Lord North's lead. Declaring Massachusetts to be in rebellion on February 9, 1775, it ordered the arrest of provincial government leaders, and authorized Gage to use force to restore British rule. Gage moved quickly once he received these instructions on April 14, 1775. Four days later he sent eight hundred troops to destroy the munitions stored at Concord, seventeen miles from Boston.

Their march did not remain a secret for long. William Dawes and Paul Revere slipped out of Boston to alert the local militia, and by dawn, when the British troops reached Lexington, about seventy of that town's militia were gathered on the common. As they heard the regulars marching into town, some militiamen urged their captain, John Parker, to abandon the common—a few dozen poorly trained militiamen were no match for eight hundred British regulars. But Parker ordered, "Stand your ground! Don't fire unless fired upon! But if they want to have a war let it begin here!"

Parker had second thoughts as the British forces massed in front of his men. "Disperse, you rebels," an officer shouted, "damn you, throw down your arms and disperse." Parker ordered his men to disperse. Some men began to move off, but others had not heard the order. In the confusion, as more British soldiers joined the line, and others moved to the militia's left, a shot rang out. No one knows who—militiaman, British soldier, or bystander—fired that first shot, but the British opened fire. Few militiamen had time to fire as they fled from the British, leaving eight of their comrades dead on the common. One British soldier was wounded. The regulars marched on to Concord.

They did not find much in Concord. Alerted to the regulars' approach, the rebels hid their supplies. The British destroyed three cannon, threw some bullets into a pond, and built a bonfire of gun carriages in front of Concord's town house. When the bonfire threatened to spread, the soldiers helped the locals protect the town house.

Captain Walter Laurie's detachment moved north of town. At the North Bridge over the Concord River, they met five hundred militiamen from Bedford, Carlisle, Stowe, Lincoln, and Acton, who had heard the alarm early in the morning and marched toward Concord. Now in perfect formation, this militia unit joined a Concord unit on the hill sloping down to the North Bridge. As the Americans neared the bridge, two more British units came to join Laurie. In the confusion the British fired across the river. Though two Americans fell dead, the rest continued advancing. Major John Buttrick of Concord, whose family had farmed the field since 1638, shouted "Fire, fellow soldiers, for God's sake fire!"

Buttrick's men returned the fire. To their surprise, the British began retreating toward Concord. The British had no reason to push on—they had destroyed the munitions—but to both American militia and British troops, the sight of British soldiers retreating under fire was a novelty. The emboldened militia pursued them. By this time the alarm had spread further, bringing fresh militia from eastern Massachusetts as well as New Hampshire and Rhode Island. Six different New England militia units attacked as the regulars retreated from Concord to Lexington, and the entire retreat to Boston was a torment to the British. From behind walls, houses, and trees, the Americans fired at the British column, or waited in quickly organized ambushes to attack the soldiers. "We retired for 15 miles under an incessant fire," reported Lord Hugh Percy, "which like a moving circle surrounded and followed us wherever we went."

By the time the British reached the safety of Charlestown, sixty-five men were dead, 180 wounded, and another twenty-seven missing. The Americans had lost fifty men, with thirty-nine wounded and five missing. Worse than being drubbed by men they regarded as a peasant rabble, the regulars now found themselves surrounded by fifteen thousand New England militiamen, who camped in Cambridge, northwest of Boston, and to the south in Roxbury, cutting Gage's troops off from supplies of food and firewood.

Elsewhere in New England, militia rallied. Benedict Arnold, a Connecticut merchant and sea captain, led a group of volunteers north to Lake Champlain. There he joined with Ethan Allen's militia, the Green Mountain Boys—formed to defend Vermont from New York's encroachments—and surprised the British garrison at Fort Ticonderoga on May 9, demanding surrender of the fort and its cannon. When the surprised British commander asked to whom he was surrendering, Allen replied, "In the name of the great Jehovah, and the Continental Congress."

The Continental Congress reconvened the day after Allen's audacious capture, but no delegates were aware of this victory. They knew about Lexington and Concord, which seemed to be Britain's answer to their petitions. Washington signaled that the time for petitioning had passed by wearing his military uniform as colonel of the Virginia regiment to Congress. Adams proposed that Congress adopt the militiamen around Boston as a Continental Army, then nominated Washington to command it. His cousin Samuel seconded the motion, and Washington accepted on the stipulation he serve without pay. Washington left for Cambridge, where he would take command of the militia forces—now the Continental Army—on July 3, 1775.

What was this Continental Army fighting for? Congress adopted a Declaration of the Causes and Necessity of Taking up Arms, reiterating loyalty to the king, but insisting on the fundamental right of the people to govern themselves. Some leaders in Congress, such as John Dickinson, were not prepared to go further. John Adams compared Congress to a "large Fleet sailing under convoy. The fleetest Sailors must wait for the dullest and slowest." But the fleet's destination was still a mystery.

Britain had a clearer aim—restoring colonial loyalty—but no clear strategy for achieving it. Some British military advisors favored a blockade, though they had neither ships nor time to do this effectively. If their navy patrolled North America, France and Spain would threaten British territories in the West Indies, India, and even Britain itself. Direct military force, without a blockade, would require at least twenty thousand men— more than were available in Britain. Fundamental disagreements among government ministers, between the ministers and the British commanders, and among the generals in America stymied the war effort. Strategists disagreed about how to win the war, but all agreed that most Americans outside New England were loyal to Britain. Isolate New England, and Britain could secure the loyalty of the rest of the Americans.

By now three more British generals had arrived in Boston. William Howe replaced Gage as commander in chief; Henry Clinton came as second in command (and would ultimately succeed Howe); John Burgoyne came as well. Howe, Clinton, and Burgoyne disagreed about everything except that Gage had been too conciliatory. Perhaps he had. Clinton believed that Gage's American wife, Margaret Kemble Gage, was a conduit for information to the rebels. Though the allegations have never been proven, Mrs. Gage, like most Americans, was torn in her loyalties.

Howe also was torn. Running for Parliament in 1774, he had opposed the ministerial policies, which he charged were bringing on a war against the Americans, a war he had pledged not to fight. His brother George had died leading Massachusetts troops in the Seven Years' War, and his family cherished the fact that Massachusetts had contributed to George Howe's Westminster Abbey monument. His sister Catherine had arranged informal peace talks between their brother Richard, the admiral, and the American agent Benjamin Franklin. Now Howe was in Boston to direct a war whose end was to restore American loyalty. He thought an overwhelming show of force would scatter the American militia; after that the New Englanders could be reconciled.

Henry Clinton saw the matter differently. Instead of reconciling New Englanders, the British should isolate them. Instead of Boston, their base should be New York, a city he knew well since his father had been its governor for ten years. Ten thousand British troops could protect the loyal subjects in the middle colonies, while ten thousand more moved down from Canada along Lake Champlain and the Hudson, rallying Loyalists and the Iroquois, and cutting off New England. This solution would require twenty thousand troops and a naval blockade. Clinton thought an alternative would be to withdraw British forces to Canada and Florida. A taste of the "anarchy and confusion which must naturally be their lot" would convince Americans that rebellion was folly.

Howe and Clinton disagreed on long- and short-term goals, but also found a situation in Boston they had not anticipated. When they left England they did not know that an American army surrounded Boston and controlled the countryside. With Cape Cod whaleboats, the rebels scoured the harbor islands of sheep and hogs, leaving British forces to subsist on salted meat. When a British foraging party brought back from far-off Connecticut some badly needed cows, the local press mocked them:

> In days of yore the British troops
> Have taken warlike kings in battle;
> But now, alas! their valor droops,
> For Gage takes naught but—harmless cattle.

Still, the newly arrived generals were optimistic. "Let us get in," Burgoyne said when told of the British soldiers' cramped quarters on Boston's narrow peninsula, "and we will soon find elbow room." Establishing himself in John Hancock's elegant Beacon Hill mansion, Clinton advised that the best elbow room would be Dorchester Neck to the south, the highest point in the surrounding area. Control of the heights would give the British command of the harbor, Castle Island, and the towns of Boston, Dorchester, and Roxbury. But, certain the rebels could not hold Dorchester Heights, the British left them unfortified.

Clinton on June 16 observed rebels moving onto Bunker Hill in Charlestown, the highest point to Boston's north. British forces had begun fortifying Bunker Hill in April, but Gage had called them off, not thinking the rebels would use the hill for an attack on Boston.

Clinton and Howe now urged an immediate attack. The next morning, June 17, the British forces began their assault to disperse the rebels from Bunker Hill, then drive the rebels from their camps in Cambridge, and cross the Charles River to drive the rebels from Roxbury. This three-day campaign would disperse the rebel militia and give the British forces their badly needed elbow room. As regulars were ferried to Charlestown that morning, others baked bread and roasted meat for the expedition.

It was early afternoon on a sweltering June day when the regulars were ready on the Charlestown shore. After his men finished dinner, at about three, Howe had the well-prepared soldiers begin a slow march up Breed's Hill, just to the south of Bunker Hill. From its summit they would be able to see the rebel fortifications on Bunker Hill.

They never had the chance. As the British line reached the top of Breed's Hill, a furious raking fire erupted from a redoubt buried on the summit. This Breed's Hill redoubt had not existed the previous day. Now it was filled with New England militiamen, who aimed low, targeted officers, and held their fire until they were sure of a hit. Legend has it that Captain Thomas Prescott shouted, "Don't fire until you see the whites of their eyes!" The first lines of British infantry took heavy casualties and quickly retreated to the base of the hill.

Howe ordered another assault. Stepping over the wounded and dead, the British troops reached the top, but again the well-aimed fire turned them back.

From Copp's Hill in Boston, Burgoyne saw snipers in Charlestown picking off British soldiers as they advanced. He had artillery lob incendiary bombs into Charlestown, setting it ablaze. General Clinton had himself rowed across to lead more men into battle. For the third assault the regulars left their packs at the base and quickly marched to the top.

Now nearly out of ammunition, the defenders decided to give up Breed's Hill and Bunker Hill but save their army to fight again. Gathering the remaining ammunition, a cadre of men prepared to stall the British while the rest retreated to Cambridge. On the third assault the British troops stormed the battlements with bayonets fixed, attacking the remaining defenders who now were out of ammunition. This final and brutal assault won the day—the British flag flew over Bunker Hill and Breed's Hill. But more than a thousand British soldiers and officers were dead or wounded, the rest could not move beyond Charlestown, and the American army survived. Rhode Islander Nathanael Greene wished the Americans could sell the British another hill at the same price.

A defeat for the Americans, Bunker Hill had nevertheless proven they could fight and left Howe and the British with a new respect for their enemy. On June 16 Breed's Hill was a pasture; the next day its fortification held off two British assaults. If the Americans could do this overnight, what must they have done in Cambridge or Roxbury? Colonel James

Abercrombie reported that idle reports among his men were "magnified to such a degree that the rebels are seen in the air carrying cannon and mortars on their shoulders." Howe would be wary of assaulting any position the Americans had time to fortify.

Howe, Clinton, and Burgoyne realized that Boston, politically and militarily, was a poor British base. Their best option was to leave, but the British government had sent them to win the war, not give up territory, and would not tolerate a sudden evacuation. Through the winter they stayed in Boston, as the Americans gained elsewhere. Richard Montgomery led an American army up Lake Champlain, and occupied Montreal while Benedict Arnold besieged Quebec. Virginia's rebel militia defeated British regulars and their Loyalist allies, forcing Lord Dunmore, the royal governor, to take refuge on a British warship. In Parliament, Charles James Fox noted that though the British held Boston, they were besieged there and in Quebec, their governor had been exiled from Virginia, and the Americans already held Montreal. Neither William Pitt, he declared, nor Alexander the Great, nor Julius Caesar, in all their wars had gained as much territory as Lord North had lost in one campaign.

From his vessel on the Chesapeake, Dunmore declared martial law and offered freedom to slaves who would rise against their rebellious masters. A desperate act, it still threatened the slave-holding Virginians. A South Carolinian told John Adams that a British officer promising "Freedom to all the Negroes who would join his Camp," could quickly enlist twenty-thousand blacks in Georgia and South Carolina. "The Negroes have a wonderfull Art of communicating Intelligence among themselves. It will run severall hundreds of Miles in a Week or Fortnight," though the British knew in case of emancipation "the Slaves of the Tories would be lost as well as those of the Whiggs," and did not want rebellion among their own West Indian slaves, on whose labor the sugar economy depended.

British authority in America crumbled as 1775 came to a close. The king proclaimed the colonies all to be in a state of rebellion, and Parliament forbade trade with the colonies, declared them out of British protection, and threatened to seize any American ships found on the high seas. Dunmore sent a raiding party ashore on the first day of 1776 to burn Norfolk. Banning trade and burning towns would not restore the inhabitants' loyalty.

Could the generals subdue the rebels? Or would a more conciliatory ministry that would not tax the Americans replace Lord North? Could the militia surrounding Boston maintain a siege through the winter, or would they return to their homes? If they went home, would they willingly return to the siege in the spring? Neither side, rebel or British, had a clear end in sight. Was the aim reconciliation? Or subjugation? Or was it independence?

Clarification came in the second week of January, 1776, in the fifty pages of an anonymous pamphlet. *Common Sense* forcefully argued that the united colonies should break with the British crown. Americans had nothing to gain, and everything to lose, by remaining in the British Empire, and Americans had the resources to defeat the greatest military power in the world. Independence was not only possible, the pamphlet argued, but necessary.

Common Sense looked to the future, not the past. It did not recite the history of the years since 1763 or dwell on the colonists' grievances. The cause was not merely America's.

> The sun never shone on a cause of greater worth. 'Tis not the affair of a city, a county, a province, or a kingdom; but of a continent—of at least one eighth part of the habitable globe. 'Tis not the concern of a day, a year, or an age; posterity are virtually involved in the contest, and will be more or less affected even to the end of time, by the proceedings now....O! ye that love mankind! Ye that dare oppose not only the tyranny but the tyrant, stand forth! Every spot of the old world is overrun with oppression. Freedom hath been hunted round the globe. Asia and Africa have long expelled her. Europe regards her like a stranger, and England hath given her warning to depart. O! receive the fugitive, and prepare in time an asylum for all mankind.

America and England had to part. Americans could not remain tied to Europe, because the English government, though better than the despotisms of France or Spain, still with its monarchy and aristocracy put up artificial barriers to the full enjoyment of the rights of man. They needed new governments based not on Europe's antiquated systems but on their own ideals.

"We have it in our power to begin the world over again." Not "since the days of Noah" had people had such an opportunity. "The birthday of a new world is at hand, and a race of men, perhaps as numerous as all Europe contains, are to receive their portion of freedom from the events of a few months."

By March, 120,000 copies of *Common Sense* had been sold; half a million copies were in print by year's end. The author did not remain anonymous for long. Thomas Paine had arrived from England just a year earlier, leaving behind a failed marriage and a failed career as an excise-tax officer. Carrying a letter of introduction from Franklin, he found work in Philadelphia writing magazine pieces. With *Common Sense* he changed the political dynamic in America.

As the anonymous author Thomas Paine changed the political dynamic, in New England an unknown former book seller, Henry Knox, shifted the military dynamic. Now an officer in Washington's army, Knox trekked to Fort Ticonderoga late in 1775. With a train of oxen, Knox and his men dragged Ticonderoga's heavy artillery, captured by Allen and Arnold in the spring, across the frozen roads and rivers of Massachusetts. He delivered them to Washington in Cambridge in February. While Washington's Cambridge batteries fired on Boston from the north, General John Thomas, a physician turned soldier, brought the cannon from Roxbury to Dorchester Heights on the bitterly cold night of March 4, 1776, fortifying the heights General Clinton had urged the British to seize in June 1775.

When the sun rose on March 5, Howe and the British forces saw a fortress on what the day before was a barren hilltop. Expecting Howe to storm Dorchester Heights, Washington asked the "men of Boston" if they would allow a British triumph on that day—the Fifth of March—the anniversary of the Boston Massacre. The men were ready for an attack that never came—a northeast storm brought snow and wind and made a British attack impossible. Wary of another victory as costly as Bunker Hill, and recognizing that Boston was not an effective base to restore colonial loyalty, Howe ordered his forces to evacuate Boston. On March 17, 1776, the British army and fleet, along with several thousand Massachusetts Loyalists, left the town, and civil government was restored.

Washington anticipated that Howe and his army would sail for New York. As soon as the last British soldiers were on their transports, Washington ordered his own men to begin their march to New York to secure its harbor. Howe and his forces sailed for New York by way of Halifax, Nova Scotia, where they put the exiled Loyalists ashore.

While the British were evacuating Boston, Henry Clinton was trying to preserve the loyal provinces of Georgia and the Carolinas. He had arrived off North Carolina in March, expecting to be met by six thousand Scottish Highlanders from the North Carolina Piedmont. Instead he met only the governors of North and South Carolina, Josiah Martin and William, Lord

Congress commissioned this gold medal for Washington after the evacuation of Boston, making it the first Congressional Medal of Honor. Washington is on the front; the reverse is the view of Boston from Dorchester Heights. (Image courtesy of the Massachusetts Historical Society.)

Campbell, respectively. The rebel militia had beaten the Highlanders at Moore's Creek Bridge, near present day Wilmington, North Carolina. Martin and Campbell assured Clinton of the Carolinas' continuing loyalty even as they asked for refuge on his warship. Clinton put his governors ashore on an island, to await the rising of their loyal people, while their slaves caught fish and foraged for wild cabbages to feed them.

Reinforcements arrived in April, along with new instructions from George Germain, the secretary of state for American affairs, who believed the loyal Carolinas and Georgia would not need Clinton. He was to return to Boston to assist Howe. Clinton thought Germain's plan "chimerical" and "false," because there were not enough "friends of government" in Georgia or the Carolinas to "defend themselves when the troops are withdrawn." Any Loyalists he mobilized would "be sacrificed" to the patriots when he left; neither knew that Howe had already abandoned Boston.

Still, Clinton obeyed, sailing in June for Charleston, South Carolina. First he would take Sullivan's Island, the poorly defended key to Charleston harbor. But bad weather kept him at sea, and by the time wind and tide shifted in his favor, the rebel militia had fortified the island. Clinton's local intelligence suggested that he take undefended Long Island, separated from Sullivan's Island only by a narrow stretch of water. Clinton's men could easily cross at low tide, when his sources told him the water was only knee deep. But the channel was seven feet deep. The men floundered under heavy fire from Sullivan's Island before retreating to their ships. They tried another attack on Sullivan's Island, but though their artillery pounded the rebel defenses, the local militia again repulsed them. Humiliated, and mocked by the Carolina militia, Clinton sailed to join Howe, now on his way to New York.

British strategists knew they needed more men than England could provide. Clinton thought Russians would be ideal soldiers in America—tough, able to withstand a variety of climates, and best of all, they could not speak English and were thus unlikely to desert. But Catherine the Great politely refused, telling George III she would not want to imply that he could not put down his own rebellions. So the British turned to the states of Germany. As elector of Hanover, George III lent five of his German battalions to himself as the king of England. He sent these Germans to garrison Minorca and Gibraltar, replacing their British regiments who sailed for America. Hanoverians stayed in Europe, but troops the British leased from Hesse-Cassel and Brunswick were sent to America. Hesse-Cassel provided twelve thousand soldiers and thirty-two cannon; the Landgrave of Hesse-Cassel received the pay and expenses of these soldiers, plus £110,000 for each year of their service and for one year after they returned home. One of every four able-bodied Hessian men fought in America. The Duke of Brunswick sent seven thousand soldiers, receiving £15,000 for every year they served and £30,000 annually for two years after their return.

The king and prime minister were determined to restore their American subjects' loyalty. The loss of Boston, the exile of governors by supposedly loyal subjects, and the American occupation of Montreal made this restoration more difficult, but not less likely. The Americans had surprised but not defeated the British forces. Nor had the Americans built the ships or made the weapons they would need to defeat the British and German troops. But loyalty and good will are not fostered by military force. The British had not adopted the best methods to achieve their goal of loyal submission.

On the American side, the goal still was not clear. Was it independence, as Thomas Paine and John Adams insisted? Or was it Parliament's disavowal of its intrusive power over them? The first question raised too many others to seem viable; the second seemed even less likely, as Parliament hired German mercenaries to enforce its will.

CHAPTER 3

INDEPENDENCE

BY SPRING 1776 BRITISH AUTHORITY HAD COLLAPSED IN ALL of the colonies. Provincial congresses and committees of safety, mainly composed of members of the suspended colonial assemblies, took on the tasks of administration. But, having begun the rebellion because Parliament exceeded its powers, these men were wary of exceeding their own. They had been created as temporary bodies—what gave them the power to tax or to demand military service? Late in 1775 Congress instructed two colonies that had asked for guidance—South Carolina, whose white minority needed a government to prevent rebellion by the black majority, and New Hampshire—to form new governments. On May 10, 1776, it called on all the colonies to create new governments. William Duane of New York said this call was "a machine for fabricating independence."

As John Adams grappled with these issues of government in Congress, he received a letter from his wife, Abigail, home in Massachusetts. "I long to hear that you have declared an independency," she wrote, "and by the way in the new Code of Laws which I suppose it will be necessary for you to make I desire you would Remember the Ladies, and be more generous and favourable to them than your ancestors." She urged him not to "put such unlimited power into the hands of Husbands," who, under the law, controlled all of a wife's property. She urged her husband to protect women from the "vicious and Lawless" who could, under the law, treat women with "cruelty and indignity."

"Remember all Men would be tyrants if they could," she said, quoting a well-known political axiom. Abigail's quote, though, was more pointedly about men than about human nature. "If perticular care and attention is not paid to the Laidies," she warned, "we are determined to foment a Rebelion, and will not hold ourselves bound by any Laws in which we have no voice, or Representation."

John's response did not please her. "As to your extraordinary Code of Laws, I cannot but laugh. We have been told that our struggle has loosened the bands of Government everywhere. That Children and Apprentices were disobedient—that schools and Colledges were grown turbulent—that Indians slighted their Guardians and Negroes grew insolent to the Masters." But her letter revealed that a more numerous and powerful group was now rising up, he thought, at the instigation of the British government. "After stirring up Tories, Landjobbers, Trimmers, Bigots, Canadians, Indians, Negroes, Hanoverians, Hessians, Russians, Irish Roman Catholicks, Scotch Renegadoes, at last they have stimulated them to demand new Priviledges and threaten to rebell."

The men, he said, knew better than to repeal their "masculine system" of governing—which he said was only imaginary. This exchange reveals how complex declaring independence would be. As the Americans were taking a position not only on their connection with the British Empire but on the very basis of government, their own claims to self-government provoked critical questioning of the nature of society itself. Why were women subject to the arbitrary rule of husbands and fathers? Why, if the Americans claimed liberty as a fundamental birthright, were one out of every five Americans enslaved? What role would native people or religious dissenters have in a new political society? Declaring independence, difficult a decision though it was, would prove less complicated than resolving these other conundrums that would follow from it.

North Carolina's provincial congress instructed its delegates to Congress to vote for independence, and the towns of Massachusetts (except Barnstable), voted for independence in April 1776. Virginia's provincial congress resolved in May that "these United Colonies are, and of right ought to be, free and independent states." Richard Henry Lee introduced and John Adams seconded this resolution in Congress on June 7. Some delegates—the New Yorkers, who had been instructed not to support independence, and Delaware's John Dickinson—balked. Rather than have a bitter debate, Congress put off a vote but appointed a committee of Adams, Thomas Jefferson, Benjamin Franklin, Roger Sherman of Connecticut, and Robert Livingston of New York to draft a declaration.

Adams knew Jefferson could summarize complicated arguments quickly and gracefully, as he had in his 1774 "Summary View of the Rights of British America" and the 1775 declaration on the "Causes and Necessity of Taking Up Arms." Jefferson's aim in the declaration was not to break new philosophical ground, but to prepare a platform on which everyone in Congress, and in the states they represented, could stand. It had to be clear, not controversial, and utterly consistent with the country's prevailing mood.

The declaration begins with an explanation of the document's purpose. One group of people is preparing to separate from another, and to take their place among the world's nations. They respect the rest of the world's opinions enough to explain their reasons, beginning with a series of "self-evident" truths—basic assumptions that justify all further actions. These truths are: all men are created equal; all men have certain "inalienable rights," including "life, liberty, and the pursuit of happiness"; in order to secure these rights, people create governments, which derive their powers "from the consent of the governed"; when a government begins violating rather than protecting these rights, the people have a right to change that government or to abolish it and create a new one to protect their rights. This was all expressed in one sentence.

The next sentence observes that prudent men would not change a government for "light and transient causes," and in fact people were more likely to suffer than to change their customary systems. But when "a long train" of abuses showed that the government was attempting "to reduce them under absolute despotism," the people have a right—indeed, a duty—to "throw off such government" and create a new one to protect their fundamental rights.

Having explained the right to throw off a government before it became despotic, the declaration lists the British government's actions that now made rebellion necessary. The grievances were not surprising: since 1764 the colonists had been protesting against the acts of Parliament—the Sugar Act, the Stamp Act, Declaratory Act, the Townshend duties, the Quartering Act, the Tea Act, the Boston Port Bill, the Quebec Act, the Prohibitory Act. But the declaration shifted the blame from Parliament to the king. In fact, "Parliament" is never mentioned. All charges are against the king, and each of the twenty-seven charges begins with "he."

The king was charged with refusing to approve laws their assemblies passed, making judges dependent on the crown for their salaries, keeping standing armies in peace time, quartering troops in private homes, and protecting those soldiers "by a mock trial from punishment for any murders which they should commit" on peaceful inhabitants. This reference to the Boston massacre was somewhat ironic, since John Adams had been the counsel for the accused in that "mock trial." The list of grievances continued: the king had cut off colonial trade; he had set up the Quebec government, or, as the declaration put it, abolished "the free system of English laws" in that province (which had only recently been introduced to English law). He had taken away colonial charters and suspended legislatures. Declaring the Americans out of his protection, he had "plundered our seas, ravaged our coasts, burnt our towns, & destroyed the lives of our people," and now was sending "large armies of foreign mercenaries, to compleat the works of death, desolation & tyranny," and, as if this was not enough, he was instigating domestic insurrections by arming slaves and the "merciless Indian savages, whose known rule of warfare is an undistinguished destruction of all ages, sexes & conditions."

Congress cut the final charge in Jefferson's draft, which charged the king with waging "cruel war against human nature itself," violating the sacred rights of life and liberty of a "distant people, who never offended him" by forcing them into slavery in a distant hemisphere. The African slave trade—"this piratical warfare"—was the shameful policy of the "Christian king of Great Britain," who was so "determined to keep open a market where MEN should be bought & sold" he had vetoed their attempts to "restrain this execrable commerce."

This passage on the slave trade is far longer than any of the other charges against the king, but it concluded with a related but very different charge. Not only had the king forced Americans to buy slaves, he was now trying to get these wronged people "to rise in arms among us" and win the liberty "of which he has deprived them" by killing the Americans he had forced to buy these enslaved men and women. Jefferson accused the king of atoning for his crimes against the liberties of one people— the enslaved—by having them take the lives of another people—the colonists. Congress struck out this whole passage on slavery and the slave trade.

After this list of charges, the declaration insisted that the Americans' petitions for redress had been answered only by repeated injuries. A "prince, whose character is thus marked by every act which may define a tyrant, is unfit to be the ruler of a free people." Later in life Adams

The first printing, on July 4, 1776, of the Americans' reasons for rebelling. This document created a nation with a birth date (July 4) and a name: The United States of America. (Image courtesy of the Massachusetts Historical Society.)

thought that perhaps they should not have called George III a tyrant. George III, determined to be a "patriot king," smarted at this label. But he alone was not to blame. Americans had "warned" the British people of attempts by "their legislature"—a reference to Parliament—"to extend an unwarrantable jurisdiction over us." But the British people had been deaf to "the voice of justice and consanguinity," so Americans had no choice but to "hold them, as we hold the rest of mankind, enemies in war, in peace friends."

For all these reasons, the declaration stated, the united colonies "are, and of right ought to be, free and independent states," absolved from all allegiance to the British crown. It concluded by announcing that all connection between the people of the colonies and the state of Great Britain was totally dissolved.

Congress voted in favor of independence on July 2; two days later, it adopted the declaration. Printer John Dunlap published five hundred copies to distribute throughout the country. At the top are the words, "In Congress, July 4, 1776." The document is titled "A Declaration by the Representatives of the United States of America, in General Congress Assembled." Prominently appearing in one bold line were the words "UNITED STATES OF AMERICA," appearing in print for the first time. The new country had a name.

Bells rang and cannon fired after the people of Philadelphia heard independence declared on July 8. The militia paraded and tore down symbols of royal authority after the reading. Throughout the country, as the people heard the declaration read in public gatherings, they reacted the same way, ringing bells, firing cannon, and tearing down royal symbols. Washington on July 9 had the declaration read to his troops in New York. Then his soldiers and the people of New York together pulled down the statue of George III and cut it to pieces. The women—both New Yorkers and the women following the army—melted the king's statue down into bullets.

Bullets they would need. As the declaration was being read on Manhattan, thirty-thousand British troops, the largest European force ever deployed outside Europe, were coming ashore on Staten Island. Washington knew his poorly armed and poorly trained New England soldiers could not defend New York from the army commanded by General William and the navy under his brother, Admiral Sir Richard Howe. Washington also had learned that the Americans had failed in Canada. The French along the St. Lawrence too well remembered New England's wars against them, and the able British governor, General Sir Guy Carleton, rallied them to break the American siege of Quebec, then beat them at Trois-Rivières. By June the badly depleted Americans—ravaged by smallpox and a Canadian winter—were retreating from Montreal.

Washington realized New York was indefensible. To hold the city of twenty-two thousand at the lower tip of Manhattan, he would also have to hold Brooklyn, whose heights loomed across the East River. To hold Brooklyn he would have to defend all of Long Island. With only nineteen thousand men, and no boats, this was impossible. Washington realized this; more important, so did General Howe. He sent Clinton on August 22 to Long Island's south shore. American Loyalists thronged to support Clinton's landing; no American rebels opposed him. Quickly Clinton's German and British troops killed or captured fourteen hundred American troops, as the rest fled to their stronghold at Brooklyn. The Battle of Long Island, the largest-scale battle in the entire Revolutionary War, was a disaster for the Americans.

Half of Washington's army was now trapped in Brooklyn. Howe could easily destroy it and crush the rebellion. But, hoping to avoid unnecessary casualties both of his own men and the deluded Americans, he decided on a siege of Brooklyn. Clinton advised him to seize Kings Bridge over the Harlem River, before Washington's Manhattan troops escaped into the Bronx. But Howe was more interested in lower Manhattan, where his brother's fleet could dock, and also in reconciliation. At any rate, a violent storm prevented any action, and the next day a dense fog shrouded New York.

Storm and fog kept the Howes from maneuvering their ships or men, which gave Washington a desperate chance. He found boats, and under cover of fog, the Americans slipped out of their fortifications in Brooklyn to be ferried across the East River. When the fog cleared, all of Washington's forces were on Manhattan. Their annihilation postponed, they had a faint chance to escape up the Hudson or into New Jersey.

On reaching New York Admiral Richard Howe had written to Franklin, proposing they meet to discuss reconciliation. They had met in 1774, over games of chess at Catherine Howe's London home, and discussed ways to protect what Franklin called "that fine and noble China Vase the British Empire." Franklin now asked if Howe remembered the "Tears of Joy that wet my Cheek" when Howe suggested "that a Reconciliation might soon take place." In response to Howe, Franklin said reconciliation was now impossible. Franklin hoped for peace between the two countries—not among people of one country. Howe should resign his command rather than pursue a war he knew to be unwise and unjust.

After the American debacle on Long Island, Howe sent captured American general John Sullivan to Philadelphia to propose that Congress send someone to discuss reconciliation. Sullivan reported enthusiastically that Howe could have the Declaratory Act set aside. John Adams opposed negotiating with Howe, wishing that "the first ball that had been fired on the day of the defeat of our army [on Long Island] had gone through [Sullivan's] head." Congress sent Adams, Franklin, and Edward Rutledge to meet the admiral on Staten Island.

The "thoughtless dissipation" of the American officers and soldiers "straggling and loitering" in New Jersey did not make Adams hopeful. Howe had sent an aide to greet them in New Jersey; this aide was to stay behind as a hostage, guaranteeing that the American envoys would not be arrested while in the British camp. Adams thought it "childish" not to trust Howe, and insisted that the officer cross to Staten Island with them. Howe's face brightened when he saw their trust, and told the Americans their trust "was the most sacred of Things."

This was the high point of the three-hour meeting. Howe supplied "good Claret, good Bread, cold Ham, Tongues, and Mutton," but said he could consider his guests only as influential citizens, not as a committee of Congress. "Your Lordship may consider me, in what light you please," John Adams said quickly, "and indeed I should be willing to consider myself, for a few moments, in any Character which would be agreeable to your Lordship, except that of a *British Subject.*"

"Mr. Adams is a decided Character," Howe said to Franklin and Rutledge. They replied that they had come to listen. Howe outlined his proposal—if the Americans resumed their allegiance to the king, the king would pardon them for rebelling. (Adams learned later that this amnesty did not include him.) Rutledge spoke up: after two years of anarchy, the states had created new governments; it was now too late for reconciliation.

Howe spoke of his own gratitude to Massachusetts for the Westminster Abbey monument it commissioned to honor his brother, and he now "felt for America, as for a Brother, and if America should fall, he should feel and lament it, like the loss of a Brother."

"We will do our Utmost Endeavours," Franklin assured him with a smile and a bow, "to save your Lordship that mortification."

As the three commissioners made their way back to Philadelphia, the Howes began their attack on Washington. Four days after the conference the British held New York City, the beginning of a seven-year occupation. Washington with five thousand men held the high ground of northern Manhattan. On either side of the Hudson, on the New Jersey Palisades and what is now known as Washington Heights, his men built Fort Lee and Fort Washington.

Meanwhile Carleton moved down from Canada, destroying the American vessels trying to hold Lake Champlain. By mid-October he held Crown Point, just a dozen miles north of Ticonderoga. Taking Ticonderoga would give him control of the Hudson. He would trap Washington between his Canadian army and Howe's forces in New York.

"Whenever an army composed as this of the rebels is has once felt itself in a situation so alarming, it can never recover," General Clinton wrote. The British strategy was destroying Americans' confidence in themselves and in Washington. "It loses all confidence in its chief; it trembles whenever its rear is threatened."

The British moved up the East River, through the treacherous currents of Hell Gate, and into the Long Island Sound Narrows, landing their forces on Throggs Neck. They anticipated losing hundreds of men in this maneuver but only lost two boats, gaining access to Westchester County. Washington moved from Harlem to White Plains. The British attacked at the end of October, squeezing the remaining eleven thousand Americans into a narrow tract divided by the Hudson and Harlem Rivers, between Harlem and Peekskill. Washington crossed the Hudson to Hackensack, New Jersey.

Howe sent General Charles Cornwallis to protect New Jersey's loyal farmers, whom he would need to provision his army in New York; and though Clinton advised taking Philadelphia, Howe instead sent him to Newport, Rhode Island—unlike the rivers near New York Harbor, Narragansett Bay rarely froze, and the fleet would need a winter anchorage. The year had begun with Washington surrounding the British in Boston; as it neared its end he was himself surrounded in Westchester, with the Howes confidently waiting for Carleton and his Canadians to come down the Hudson to finish in one stroke the American army and rebellion.

But Carleton did not arrive. Benedict Arnold had built a small fleet of gunboats on Lake Champlain that kept Carleton from Ticonderoga. Carleton's long Canadian experience taught him not to stay in Crown Point over the winter; his military experience told him not to stretch his supply lines too far. He retreated to Canada in November.

Even without Carleton, Howe pushed the remaining Americans out of Manhattan. Johann Gottlieb Rall's Hessians took Fort Washington and nearly two thousand prisoners on December 16. Two days later they crossed the Hudson and drove the Americans from Fort Lee. The "rebels fled like scared rabbits," a British officer wrote, "leaving some poor pork, a few greasy proclamations, and some of that scoundrel 'Common Sense' man's letters; which we can read at our leisure, now that we have got one of 'the impregnable redoubts' of Mr. Washington to quarter in."

Paine had joined the army at Fort Lee, one of the few new recruits in a rapidly disappearing army. Washington had nineteen thousand men with him in New York; barely three thousand were still with him when he reached the Delaware. Just ahead of Cornwallis, he commandeered all of

German-born artist Emanuel Leutze (1816–1868) spent most of his first twenty-four years in America, before returning to Germany to study art. He began this heroic painting, *Washington Crossing the Delaware*, which is twelve feet high and twenty-one feet long, in 1848, the year of European revolutions. Washington and his diverse group—backwoodsmen and gentlemen, a black sailor from New England, a Native American, and one androgynous figure who might be a woman—embark across the icy river. Leutze hoped to inspire Europeans with the example of Washington and the American cause. Henry James called this copy, which Leutze sent to America in 1851, an "epoch-making masterpiece"; Leutze returned to America in 1859, but the original painting stayed in Germany, where a British bomber destroyed it in 1942. (Image courtesy of the Metropolitan Museum of Art.)

the boats on the Delaware's New Jersey banks and crossed into Pennsylvania. Congress fled to Baltimore.

On the same day Washington retreated across the Delaware, the British captured Charles Lee, the one American general they recognized. Commissioned a general in the British army, Lee, like the Howes and Cornwallis, sympathized with the American cause. Unlike them, he joined the Americans in 1776. Because he had been a British officer, his former comrades regarded Lee as the only competent American general. Separated from his troops on December 12, Lee spent the night at a New Jersey inn, tarried the next morning, and was still not dressed at eleven when a British scouting party captured him.

Having captured Lee and driven Washington out of New York and New Jersey, Howe could let his men rest over the winter. The British and Hessians set up posts to protect New Jersey. Colonel Rall occupied Trenton, and Howe put most of his army into winter quarters in New York. Cornwallis, confident that the rebellion was collapsing and the war would be over by spring, prepared to sail home.

"These are the times that try men's souls," Thomas Paine wrote as the dwindling army fled across New Jersey. "The summer soldier and the sunshine patriot will, in this crisis, shrink from the service of their country; but he that stands it now deserves the love and thanks of man and woman. Tyranny, like hell, is not easily conquered.... Heaven knows how to put a proper price upon its goods; and it would be strange indeed if so celestial an article as FREEDOM should not be highly rated."

Paine recalled a tavern keeper in Amboy who stood at his door talking politics, with his small child by his side. The father concluded his political discourse, "*Well! Give me peace in my day.*" Paine was outraged. The man was hardly a father at all—"a generous parent should have said, '*If there must be trouble, let it be in my day, that my child may have peace.*'"

Paine brushed off the loss of New York and reminded the citizens of New Jersey that a fifteenth-century British army that ravaged France was "driven back like men petrified with fear" by an army headed by a woman, Joan of Arc. "Would that heaven might inspire some Jersey maid to spirit up her countrymen, and save her fair fellow sufferers from ravage and ravishment!"

Paine's message was not for the leaders of the army or Congress. It was for the ordinary men and women of America. This was not Washington's or Congress's cause, it was theirs. "Say not that thousands are gone, turn out your tens of thousands; throw not the burden of the day upon

Providence, but '*show your faith by your works*,' that God may bless you." This was their crisis—it would be their loss, or their opportunity. "Let it be told to the future world, that in the depth of winter, when nothing but hope and virtue could survive, that the city and the country, alarmed at one common danger, came forth to meet and repulse it."

Slipping into Philadelphia, Paine had the pamphlet printed under the title *The American Crisis.* Just as he had mustered his men in the New York summer to hear the Declaration of Independence, Washington in the Pennsylvania winter mustered them to hear *The Crisis.* He knew that his troops were disappearing. Those who remained would go home when their enlistments were up in the first week of January. No more men would join in the spring. If he did not act now, he could never act again.

In a Christmas-night snowstorm, with floes of ice surrounding the boats, Washington had his twenty-four hundred men rowed across the Delaware. Just after dawn they struck the Hessian camp in Trenton. In a quick and well-planned action Washington's men captured more than nine hundred Hessians.

This brilliant military stroke awakened Howe, and awakened New Jersey. Howe had set up posts to protect the Loyalists, but the Hessian and British soldiers were not good protectors. Seeing all Americans as rebels, the Hessians and some British treated civilians brutally, raping women and stealing property. Loyalist New Jerseyans turned against the cause the Hessians served. In Trenton, Washington's men liberated wagons of loot the Hessians had taken from New Jersey homes, souvenirs they planned to bring home, and returned the property to its rightful owners.

The Hessians turned New Jersey against the king, but Americans quickly forgave them. Washington paroled the nine hundred prisoners and sent them to the Potomac and Shenandoah valleys, where they sat out the war. Many stayed after it ended, rather than return to the dominion of the Landgrave of Hesse-Cassel. Aware that rich American land, and freedom from being hired out as mercenaries, might tempt other Germans, Franklin had Congress offer deserters land bounties. He had the offer printed in German on cards inserted into tobacco pouches sold in New York.

The victory at Trenton brought more men into Washington's camp. It also brought out the Pennsylvania and New Jersey militias to set up patrols and ambushes on the roads between Princeton and New Brunswick.

Cornwallis had been aboard a ship bound for England but came ashore to lead ten thousand men across New Jersey. Late on New Year's

Day, 1777, he reached Princeton. With a force much larger than Washington's, he planned to attack Trenton the next day. But American riflemen harassed his march, aiming at officers as the line advanced. The sun was setting by the time Cornwallis reached Trenton. The Americans moved into defensive positions south of Assunpink Creek; Cornwallis drew up his own men on the north bank, to show the Americans how badly outnumbered they were. He ordered his exhausted men to rest for the next day, when they would finally destroy Washington's army. One officer urged Cornwallis to attack that night—"If you trust those people tonight you will see nothing of them in the morning." Cornwallis reportedly answered, "We've got the Old Fox safe now. We'll go over and bag him in the morning."

The Old Fox and his own officers that night discussed their obvious dilemma—they were about to be overwhelmed by Cornwallis's army. Washington asked advice. Locals had told Arthur St. Clair, an officer in the Continental Army, about a back road to Princeton. The army could get there by dawn, attack the British rear, and control the road back to New Brunswick. Ordering five hundred men to stay in Trenton, keeping their fires blazing all night and loudly digging trenches and building fortifications, Washington and the rest of his army quietly marched away on the back roads to Princeton.

Just after dawn, as Cornwallis prepared finally to destroy Washington's army at Trenton, the American forces surprised the British at Princeton. Though the initial American lines broke when the stunned British recovered, Washington arrived, rallied his men (one soldier later reported closing his eyes so he would not see Washington fall), and led the army into Princeton.

In Trenton, Cornwallis heard the distant thunder of guns to the northwest. He turned his men around to march to Princeton. By the time he arrived, Washington and his men had defeated the rear of the British army and had moved east, hoping to capture the British supply wagons or even their base at New Brunswick. But Washington's men were exhausted from marching, fighting, and marching. He turned north to take up winter quarters in Morristown.

Cornwallis did not pursue him—he was now wary of Washington's strength and strategic sense. Despite defeats at Long Island, White Plains, Harlem, and Fort Lee, despite the humiliating retreat across New Jersey, Washington and his men kept coming back. Cornwallis ushered his own men to defend New Brunswick and Amboy. For the rest of the winter, they held these New Jersey posts, using them for foraging expeditions to feed their forces based in New York. Washington's men and the New Jersey militia spent the winter attacking these foraging parties, killing, wounding, or capturing more than nine hundred men between January and March, weakening the British forces as effectively as Trenton and Princeton had shattered their notion of invincibility.

Washington knew victory depended not on his ability to hold territory but on his army's ability to counter the superior British forces, and his army depended for survival on the support of men and women in the countryside. Howe and Clinton had been sent to achieve a political end—reconciliation—through military means. Washington was securing a military end—victory—through the political means of cultivating support from the men and women the army protected.

CHAPTER 4

WAR

FRANCE WAS MORE LIKELY TO HELP REBELS WHO COULD HELP themselves. Franklin received an enthusiastic greeting on his arrival in Paris in December. "His name was familiar to government and people, to foreign countries," John Adams wrote. "There was scarcely a peasant or a citizen, a valet, coachman, or footman, a lady's chamberlain, a scullion in the kitchen, who did not consider him a friend to humankind."

The playwright Beaumarchais formed a dummy corporation to ship muskets and gunpowder to the Americans, and King Louis XVI secretly loaned it a million livres ($200,000). Eleven thousand French muskets and one thousand barrels of gunpowder reached America in 1777; by 1783, France would send the Americans £48 million ($1.4 billion today) worth of supplies and weapons.

Weapons were essential; French officers were a problem. Eager for a chance to fight the English and for more exciting duty than a West Indian garrison, French officers sought American commissions. Some officers—particularly engineers—the Americans needed, but others were nuisances, if not dangers. Phillippe Charles Tronson du Coudray, a French artillery officer, insisted on being made major general in charge of artillery and engineers. He demanded seniority over all Americans but Washington, and Congressional salaries for his staff—a secretary, a designer, three servants, and six captains and twelve lieutenants. Silas Deane, handling American affairs in Paris before Franklin's arrival, agreed because du Coudray assured him that he could bring a hundred more French officers into the American cause.

Dr. Franklin erhält, als Gesandter des Americanischen Frey Staats, seine erste Audienz in Frankreich, zu Versailles. am 20ten Märtz 1778.

Benjamin Franklin is presented to King Louis XVI of France, who has recognized American independence and declared war on England, March 1778. (Image courtesy of the Massachusetts Historical Society.)

The promise of a hundred more du Coudrays displeased Henry Knox, Nathanael Greene, and John Sullivan, who threatened to retire if du Coudray became their superior. Congress blasted Knox, Greene, and Sullivan for self-interest and for interfering with the people's representatives; not wanting to lose their services, Congress offered du Coudray the post of inspector general. He refused angrily, insisting he be made a major general, the equal of Washington. Du Coudray also angrily refused the suggestion of a Philadelphia ferry operator that he dismount for the boat ride across the Schuylkill, insisting that French generals do not take orders from boatmen. Moving boats spook horses, and du Coudray's jumped overboard and drowned him. "Monsieur du Coudray," wrote Johann Kalb, "has just put Congress much at ease by his death."

Kalb, a Bavarian-born veteran of the French army, had visited America in the late 1760s to gather intelligence on colonial attitudes. He returned in July 1777 with another French officer, the wealthy young nobleman Marie Joseph Paul de Lafayette, nephew of France's ambassador to England. Young Lafayette, not yet twenty years old, had become enthused with the American cause. His springtime visit to London had been a sensation—"We talk chiefly of the Marquis de la Fayette," historian Edward Gibbon wrote. Despite meeting with General Henry Clinton, Lord Germaine, the king's war minister, and even King George III, who invited him to inspect naval fortifications, Lafayette did not stray from the cause. In France he purchased and outfitted a ship, and eluded his own king's order for his arrest (Louis XVI knew that allowing an important nobleman to go openly to America would bring trouble from England) to slip out of France.

Lafayette and his party landed in South Carolina, then made their way to Philadelphia, arriving just as Congress had wearied of French generals seeking ranks and paychecks. Congress did not let him into the building. It sent its only member who spoke French, James Lovell, a former teacher at Boston's Latin School, to send him away. Lafayette was persistent. Congress agreed it would do no harm to let him speak to them the next day. After summarizing in English the difficulties endured and the expenses incurred in coming to America, he concluded, "After the sacrifices I have made, I have the right to exact two favors: one is, to serve at my own expense; the other is, to serve at first as a volunteer."

A French officer wanting to serve, not command, was a novelty. Lafayette met Washington a few days later, and the two formed a professional bond and a friendship. By this time Congress had received

Franklin's testimonial to Lafayette's political importance and allowed him to stay.

The war now took a new turn. Burgoyne had proposed a new version of the strategy to cut off New England by securing Lake Champlain and the Hudson, making the case with such bluster the British ministry accepted it. Burgoyne "almost promises to cross America in a hop, step, and a jump," wrote British novelist and gossip Horace Walpole, who preferred Howe's modesty. "At least if he does nothing," Howe "does not break his word."

Burgoyne reached Canada with four thousand British and three thousand New Brunswick soldiers. Governor Carleton resigned when he learned that Burgoyne had come to do what Carleton had nearly done with fewer men the previous year. The king refused Carleton's resignation, and the governor helped Burgoyne get his forces to Lake Champlain and enlisted Canadian militia and Canadian provisions.

General John Burgoyne enlisted the support of the Iroquois for his campaign into New York by way of Canada. (Image courtesy of the Massachusetts Historical Society.)

Neither Germaine nor Burgoyne had told Howe that the plan called for Howe to send a force up the Hudson to meet Burgoyne. Howe instead was on his way to take Philadelphia. Leaving Clinton in New York, the Howes and 266 vessels sailed in early summer. No one in Canada, London, Philadelphia, or Washington's army knew where the British army had gone. "The Howes are gone the Lord knows whither," Horace Walpole wrote, "and have carried the American war with them."

In late July the fleet appeared off the Delaware, then vanished again for three weeks. Toward the end of August it was off the Chesapeake and began making its way up the bay. Washington suspected the Howes were heading to Philadelphia, but he had already sent his forces to defend New York and New England against Burgoyne.

Burgoyne found the Canadian and New York terrain more difficult than it had appeared on London maps. The force he sent to drive in along the Mohawk River never got past Fort Stanwix (now Rome, New York). The nine hundred Germans sent to forage in Vermont, marching in their cavalry boots in anticipation of riding out on fine New England horses, instead met the Vermont and New Hampshire militias at Bennington. The Germans were all killed or captured, and the New England militia moved on to Bemis Heights, near Saratoga, where Horatio Gates waited for Burgoyne's arrival. Burgoyne expected to be met on the Hudson by a British, not an American, army.

Howe now had seventeen thousand men in Pennsylvania, while Washington with eleven thousand ragged troops had to defend Philadelphia. Cornwallis and Wilhelm von Knyphausen's Hessians pinned down Washington's forces along Brandywine Creek, southwest of Philadelphia, on September 11. Greene kept Cornwallis and Knyphausen at bay long enough for Washington to retreat to Chester. Still a volunteer, Lafayette stepped in to rally an American unit breaking under the British attack. Shot in the leg, he was one of seven hundred men on the American side wounded, killed, or captured. With defeat imminent, Congress fled to York, Pennsylvania. Two weeks later, the British and Germans occupied Philadelphia.

By this time Burgoyne had lost six hundred men in an unsuccessful attack on the Americans at Bemis Heights. He tried again on October 7 and failed. He sent desperate pleas to New York for Clinton to come up the river. Clinton took the American forts on the lower Hudson but then had new orders from Howe—send two thousand men to help secure the lower Delaware. Clinton knew that Howe had overwhelmed the Americans. Why did he need reinforcements?

Howe held their capital, but Washington still had his army. Once again he surprised the British. After being defeated on the Brandywine and driven from Philadelphia, Washington on October 4 attacked the superior British force at Germantown. Though the British killed, wounded, or captured more than a thousand of Washington's men, his attack reminded Howe of Washington's tenacity. Frederick the Great thought the Americans had lost the war when they lost Philadelphia. But when he heard of Germantown, he knew that the Americans, if led by Washington, must win.

Burgoyne was in trouble on the Hudson. The New England militias closed in on Saratoga. Knowing his supply lines were stretched thin, that the force on the Mohawk was turned back, and suspecting that no aid would come from Clinton, Burgoyne on October 17 surrendered to the Americans. Five thousand British and German prisoners were brought to Boston.

The capture of Burgoyne's army and Washington's surprise attack at Germantown was evidence to France that the Americans could win. In February 1778, King Louis XVI recognized the independence of the United States. Renouncing any attempt to regain Canada, France pledged to fight until the British recognized American independence. France could send men and arms to America; more ominously for Britain, it could attack the West Indies and even England.

Lord Camden blasted Prime Minister North for starting a war believing the Americans were cowards and the French were idiots. Ships currently blockading the American coast were now needed to protect the home islands and the routes to India—they could not do all three. A French fleet—twelve ships of the line and five frigates, carrying two infantry brigades—under the admiral Comte d'Estaing, sailed from Toulon in April. By the time Britain mustered a force to pursue them, d'Estaing was halfway across the Atlantic.

Lord North saw that England had two choices: send more men and resources to conquer the Americans, or withdraw. He knew the Americans would fight until their independence was recognized; he also knew the king would never accept independence. The worst-case scenario was to do what Clinton had proposed in 1775—hold Canada, Florida, and the

West Indies, and abandon further military struggle in the rebellious colonies. But the British also held New York, Newport, and Philadelphia, bases from which to win back American loyalty.

North sent commissioners to negotiate with the Americans: the Earl of Carlisle, an opposition Whig; George Johnstone, former governor of Florida; and William Eden, head of the government's intelligence services. Parliament rescinded the Declaratory Act, promised not to tax the colonies directly, and further promised to spend revenue raised in America in America, not England. Most Americans might have accepted this in 1774. They would not in 1778.

Occupying Philadelphia gave the British an opportunity to conciliate Americans. The city's Quakers were against war in principle, while the city's Loyalists blamed their rebellious neighbors for starting this war in particular. Joseph Galloway, a longtime Philadelphia politician, former ally of Franklin, and member of the first Continental Congress (but opponent of independence), was put in charge of Philadelphia's government. Howe hoped Galloway would rally the loyal and conciliate the rebellious. But Galloway's opinion of himself and confidence in his importance were too outsized to make him effective either as an administrator or conciliator.

With Howe and the British army occupying Philadelphia, Washington and his forces spent the winter at Valley Forge, twenty miles from the city. The bitterly cold Valley Forge winter has become part of American folklore, a defining time for Washington and his army. His men faced a persistent lack of food, money, and clothing, but Washington would not allow them to despair or the army to disappear.

He put General Nathanael Greene in charge of the commissary, against Greene's wishes. This Rhode Island Quaker—expelled from the Quaker meeting for carrying arms in public—wanted to fight. Fight he had, at Bunker Hill, New York, Trenton, Princeton, and Brandywine Creek. Now Washington put him in charge of supplying food and clothing, which Greene did. The army did not starve, but it came close.

Into the camp fortuitously came Friedrich Wilhelm von Steuben, who told the Americans he was a lieutenant general under Frederick the Great. Steuben had been on the staff at Frederick's headquarters, but he had never served under him in battle. His honorary title came from a small German principality. But like Lafayette, Steuben was not asking for a salary. Washington gave him a hundred men to train; he was so impressed with the results after two weeks that he let him train another hundred. By winter's end Steuben had trained these farmers, mechanics, and artisans—drilling them, marching them, teaching them tactics. The men were already veterans; Steuben's training made them a disciplined and effective army.

With one officer to feed his army, another to train it, Washington still had to fight to maintain command over it. Some members of Congress, particularly New Englanders, wondered why Gates, the victor at Saratoga, should not replace Washington, who did little but retreat. Gates and Thomas Conway, an Irish-born French officer, schemed to replace Washington; but Washington had enough allies in Congress, and by this time in the army itself, to hold his position. Congress wanted Washington to drive the British from Philadelphia and also wanted Lafayette to invade Canada, hoping he could rally the French Canadians. Greene saw this "Don Quixote expedition to the northward" as a ploy "to increase the difficulties of the General."

Clinton arrived early in May to replace the Howes. He had new orders: to give up Philadelphia but hold New York, and to send most of his men to Florida and the Caribbean. Philadelphia's Loyalists, who had enjoyed a winter with the Howes, were thrown into a state of "Horror & melancholy." Galloway knew he would be "exposed to the Rage of his bitter Enemies, deprived of a fortune of about £70,000, and now left to wander like Cain upon the Earth without Home, & without Property."

Galloway's wife, Grace Growden Galloway, daughter of one of Pennsylvania's leading men and wife of another, remained in her home after the British evacuation. When the patriots evicted her, she maintained her dignity: "I...laughed at the whole wig party. I told them I was the happyest woman in town for I had been stripped and Turned out of Doors yet I was still the same and must be Joseph Galloways Wife and Lawrence Growdons daughter and that it was Not in their power to humble Me."

"I now look upon the Contest as at an End," Lord Howe's secretary wrote. "No man can be expected to declare for us, when he cannot be assured of a Fortnight's Protection." Desperate, the Loyalists asked Clinton's permission to negotiate with Washington. Turning down that option, knowing that it would allow every Loyalist in the country to abandon the cause, Clinton reluctantly agreed to take the Loyalists with him.

The Loyalists and the British officers blamed Clinton, but wanted to recognize the Howes. They planned a "meschianza," with fireworks, a parade, and a jousting tournament. British officers dressed as knights, attended by Philadelphia slaves in turbans and robes. A select few of

Philadelphia's young women dressed as Turkish princesses, carried by turbaned slaves through the streets on elaborately decorated sedan chairs. The British knights competed for their favor. A great entertainment, but as Lord Howe's secretary noted, "It cost a great Sum of Money."

Ticket for the Meschianza

While the Americans at Valley Forge built an army, British officers in Philadelphia feted their departing commander, General William Howe, with a "meschianza." (Image courtesy of the Massachusetts Historical Society.)

Our Enemies will dwell upon the Folly & Extravagance of it with Pleasure."

The three commissioners North had sent to offer terms to the Americans arrived just as the British were abandoning Philadelphia. They were stunned to find Philadelphia being abandoned. When Clinton denied them permission to meet with Congress, they asked Washington to intercede. He sent their request to Congress, but did no more. The commissioners realized their mission was one "of ridicule, nullity, and embarrassments."

Clinton left Philadelphia on June 18, with eighteen thousand men and a baggage train twelve miles long. Knowing that Washington might attack, he placed half his army in front of the baggage train, the rest behind. After fourteen hours of rain the weather turned hot and the New Jersey mosquitoes came out in large numbers. Every third Hessian collapsed from heat stroke; some did not survive. New Jersey's people, particularly women, hid from the retreating British and Germans, making farms and villages seem abandoned. But the rebellious men destroyed bridges to slow Clinton's march.

These two slow-moving armies divided by miles of luggage made tempting targets on the hot roads to New Brunswick. Washington and his officers debated what to do. Charles Lee, released from his British captivity, thought the French alliance meant certain victory, that Washington should no longer fight but rather should build Clinton a "bridge of gold" across New Jersey. Others—Greene, Steuben, Wayne, and Lafayette—urged an attack. Washington opted to send a few men to harass the retreating column; aide Alexander Hamilton said this modest plan would have "done honor to the most honorable body of midwives and to them only."

Cornwallis, with the rear of the British army, waited in pine barrens near Monmouth Courthouse (now Freehold) for the advance army and baggage to board ferries for New York. Lee, initially opposed to an attack, received permission to lead a surprise attack against the British column. Cornwallis responded quickly and forced Lee to retreat. When Washington came on the scene and demanded to know why he had ordered a retreat, Lee explained that "the attack had been made contrary to his opinion," and when it did not go well he called it off. Washington denounced him as a "damned poltroon" (coward) as he rallied the men.

Clinton hoped Washington would come to Lee's aid—he knew he could win a general engagement and finally defeat the Old Fox. But Washington knew enough to avoid a general engagement. He organized the forces to resist further British advance, holding their ground to prevent a general defeat. Monmouth was not a victory for either side; the Americans retreated, losing more than two hundred men, and Clinton's forces—minus 358 killed, wounded, or dead of heatstroke—continued on to the New York ferries. But the American army, trained over the winter at Valley Forge, fought like an army. Washington ordered Lee court-martialed and dismissed.

Just a week after the British got safely to New York, the French fleet arrived off the Delaware. Comte d'Estaing had missed catching Howe's

In the blistering heat at Monmouth, women—often wives or girlfriends of soldiers, and nicknamed "Molly Pitcher"—carried water to cool both the men and the guns. When gunner William Hays was wounded, his wife, Mary Ludwick Hays, put down her bucket and took his place at the gun. She had been with her husband and the army through Valley Forge; he would receive a land grant, and she would later receive a pension for her service and a place in American history as "Molly Pitcher." (Image courtesy of the Massachusetts Historical Society.)

fleet at sea or blockading it in the Delaware. He now had them bottled up in New York. Admiral Howe thought the French would attack New York; Clinton watched Washington's move across the Hudson north of the city and anticipated an attack on the British at Newport.

Clinton was right. While the British fortified New York, d'Estaing sailed for Narragansett Bay. There John Sullivan and American militia joined the French forces, who landed to besiege Newport. The British sank their own ships in Newport's harbor to stymie a French assault. They were certain to starve while Howe waited in New York patiently for an attack. But d'Estaing sailed off to fight another British fleet that appeared off Rhode Island, and a hurricane struck. The besiegers tried to hold their tents and supplies in the storm that battered the French fleet, which returned finally to take the drenched French soldiers to dry out in Boston. D'Estaing repaired his fleet in Boston, then sailed to the Caribbean.

Sullivan was furious. Why not repair the ships in Providence, where they could still support the siege of Newport? He blamed d'Estaing for abandoning his men and cause, while Loyalists mocked this first combined American-French campaign:

> As Jonathan so much desired
> To shine in martial story,
> D'Estaing with politeness retired
> To leave him all the glory...
>
> To stay, unless he rul'd the sea,
> He thought would not be right, sir,
> And Continental troops, said he,
> On islands should not fight, sir.

But d'Estaing took his Continental troops to fight on islands, in the Caribbean. He and Clinton were more interested in the West Indies than Rhode Island. Clinton sent the British fleet to the Caribbean at the same time as d'Estaing sailed. Neither fleet spied the other as they sailed side by side for the West Indies. Washington, still without a naval force, kept the British garrisons pinned down in New York and Newport.

Clinton had not given up on North America. He believed in the loyalty of the Carolinas and Georgia. In December 1778 the British forces made their way up the Savannah River on flat boats, encountering only token resistance (barely thirty men manned the strong post on the bluffs downriver from Savannah). The rebels tried to flee as the British took

Savannah, capturing forty rebel officers and five hundred men. The civilians fled, but most quickly returned to pledge their loyalty. One Loyalist officer said they saw "Money and Property as Greater Goods than Rebellion and Poverty." With Savannah as a base, the British restored Georgia's royal government and threatened Charleston.

Retaking Georgia and holding New York and Newport, though, were not signs of impending British victory. Spain declared war on England in April 1779, not to help Americans but to retake Gibraltar and weaken Britain in the West Indies and North America. French and Spanish warships patrolled the English Channel and threatened to invade England itself while her armies were across the Atlantic. A London journalist wrote that the British ministry had "created a war with America, another with France, a third with Spain, and now a fourth with Holland....The candle they have lighted in America may, and probably will, make a dreadful fire in Europe."

The fire in Europe came from the sea. The Americans turned their merchant fleet into privateers and between 1775 and 1778 took about a thousand British ships. With Spain and France in the war, their annual captures doubled as Spanish and French ports opened to their prizes. Washington lacked sea power to transport troops or support military actions; but Americans did not shy from the sea. Ship owners, crews, and captains found privateering more lucrative than blockading, transporting, or bombarding.

John Paul Jones, on the sloop *Ranger* in 1778, raided English and Scottish coastal towns, and even captured a British warship in Britain's home waters. A former British merchant captain, Jones sailed the *Providence* in August 1776 to attack British merchant ships in the West Indies, becoming the first captain to raise an American flag on a warship. France outfitted Jones with a privateer, naming it *Bonhomme Richard* (Poor Richard) in Franklin's honor. In late summer 1779 he attacked a British merchant convoy in the North Sea. In a furious battle the British warship *Serapis* engaged *Bonhomme Richard*. When he saw officers on the burning *Bonhomme Richard* lowering the flag, Captain Pearson of the *Serapis* asked if they surrendered. Jones replied, "I have not yet begun to fight!"

Jones instead forced Pearson to surrender, crowded his own survivors onto the *Serapis*, and left the *Bonhomme Richard* to sink as he sailed to Holland. "Humanity cannot but recoil from the prospect of such finished horror," he lamented to Franklin "that war should produce such fatal consequences." A famous American victory, it was Jones's last under the American flag.

The American ability to attack so close to the English coast and threats from Spain, France, and Holland demoralized the British public and made them question the war effort. Parliament launched an investigation that turned into an argument between supporters of the politicians such as the lord of admiralty, the Earl of Sandwich, and Secretary of State Germaine, on the one hand, and supporters of the military leaders, such as the Howe brothers, sent to carry out their policies, on the other. Politicians and soldiers blamed each other for mismanagement and incompetence.

While rebellion raged in America and a war brewed in Europe, another war erupted on the American frontier. After the sudden death of British Indian commissioner William Johnson in 1774, a calamity for Britain's alliance with the Iroquois, the Americans persuaded the powerful Iroquois to remain neutral. The Iroquois and most other Native Americans stayed out of this war among the English.

But Americans from Fort Pitt and British from Detroit tried to draw in Native warriors. The British had invited the Iroquois to "come and see them whip the rebels" at Fort Stanwix. Instead of observing, the warriors were "obliged to fight for their lives" against the Americans, and then against one another. Instead of uniting in neutrality, the Iroquois divided—Seneca, Mohawk, and Cayuga with the British, and Oneida and Tuscarora with the Americans, while the Onondaga desperately tried to stay neutral. Individuals, too, took different sides. Civil war erupted among the Iroquois when the Seneca attacked the Oneida, who attacked the Mohawks and destroyed their towns and corn fields.

Learning that neutral Onondaga diplomats had conferred with the British at Quebec, Washington determined to "carry the war into the Heart of the Country." He sent General John Sullivan to destroy the Onondaga's ability to wage war, or even survive, in the fall of 1779. Sullivan burned forty Onondaga towns and 160,000 bushels of corn, and even cut down their fruit trees. The Onondaga fled to British protection. Fearing retaliation from other Iroquois, the Oneida fled to American protection. The Iroquois alliance, founded before Europeans set foot on North America, was broken.

Simultaneous with Sullivan's campaign, a Virginia expedition attacked Shawnee towns in Ohio, and George Rogers Clarke with two hundred men captured the British fort at Vincennes. These actions devastated the Native populations and left the British holding only Detroit in the territory north of the Ohio. In the winter of 1781–82, Wyandot and Shawnee warriors attacked frontier settlements along the Ohio River. Rumors spread that the Christian Delaware, overseen by Moravian missionaries in Pennsylvania, sheltered the attackers. Pennsylvania's militia turned out in March 1782 in retaliation for the Shawnee and Wyandot attacks, seizing and massacring one hundred unarmed Delaware in what is now Ohio, including women and children.

This war continued long after the British and Americans made peace. The expeditions against the Iroquois, Miami, Shawnee, and Cherokees alerted the Americans to the agricultural richness of these territories. After the war, the rich farmlands of western New York State, Ohio, and Kentucky drew white Americans across the mountains; cash-starved states paid soldiers with grants of land wrested from the Indians. Conflict over this land would continue into the nineteenth century.

Emboldened by their attacks on Native Americans and on the British coast, in the fall of 1780 General Benjamin Lincoln, joined by the French force from the Caribbean, tried to retake Savannah from the British. But eight hundred of the five thousand French and Americans were killed, wounded, or captured in the disastrous attack. The French returned to the Caribbean, and Lincoln retreated to Charleston. With Washington in winter quarters at Morristown, New Jersey, General Clinton sailed with eight thousand men for Charleston the day after Christmas, 1780. Clinton began his siege in April, and on May 12 forced Lincoln to surrender his army and the town. Having restored South Carolina and Georgia to British control, Clinton returned to New York, leaving Cornwallis with eight thousand men to pacify the Carolinas.

The British strategy was based on the assumption that most whites in the Carolinas and Georgia were loyal. Clinton required Carolinians to swear allegiance to the Crown, a problematic policy. Captured rebels had been released on parole, with the option of simply sitting out the war. Now Clinton forced them to take sides. Some did swear loyalty to the king and were rewarded by the newly restored royal government. This made Carolinians whose loyalty had never wavered feel betrayed, as the defeated rebels regained power and fortune.

South Carolina erupted in savage guerrilla fighting, loosely following the division between patriot and Loyalist, but actually arising out of longstanding local and personal grievances. The war gave local factions a chance to settle old scores. Loyalist militias attacked the homes of paroled patriots and noncombatants, reawakening rebellion in South Carolina's backcountry.

From Augusta, Georgia, to Georgetown on Carolina's coast Cornwallis established a ring of forts. British officers Banastre Tarleton and Patrick Ferguson raised legions of Loyalists to subdue their rebellious neighbors.

Three notable South Carolina officers broke their paroles to become guerrilla fighters. By 1779 former Continental officer Thomas Sumter was paroled and living quietly on his plantation. When Tarleton's Loyalist legion burned his Waxhaws house, Sumter organized neighbors into a guerrilla band that attacked British and Loyalist forces on the Carolina frontier. Presbyterian elder Andrew Pickens, a Seven Years' War veteran, took the loyalty oath after Charleston fell. A Loyalist band raided his farm and brought him back to action. Lieutenant Colonel Francis Marion avoided capture when Charleston fell, and organized a unit of guerrillas, which another American officer described as "distinguished by small leather caps, and the wretchedness of their attire. Their numbers did not exceed twenty men and boys, some white, some black, and all mounted, but most of them miserably equipped. Their appearance was, in fact, so burlesque that it was with much difficulty that the diversion of the regular soldiers was restrained by the officers."

Marion might have seemed a burlesque diversion, but Cornwallis wrote that "Colonel Marion has so wrought on the minds of the people, partly by the terror of his threats and cruelty of his punishments, and partly by the promise of plunder, that there was scarcely an inhabitant between the Santee and the Pedee that was not in arms against us." Cornwallis attributed Marion's success to his terrorist tactics and the promise of plunder; Marion's men saw themselves as a guerrilla unit liberating South Carolina from British occupation. In either case, Marion, Pickens, and Sumter were more effective than the American regulars.

Congress, over Washington's objections, sent Horatio Gates to command what remained of the Continental Army in the South. Gates organized his four thousand regulars and militia to surprise Cornwallis's base at Camden, South Carolina. Sensing that Gates would attack there, Cornwallis was ready. Though Gates had twice the men, the British still easily routed the Americans. Gates fled to North Carolina; by the time he reached Hillsborough, 160 miles from the battle scene, fewer than seven hundred men remained in his army. Cornwallis moved into North Carolina, while South Carolina degenerated into bitter civil war between irregular bands of patriots and Loyalists.

Like South Carolina, New York's Westchester County was also bitterly divided. Loyalist partisans, called Cowboys, controlled the county's

Mason Locke Weems, who created the story of George Washington cutting down a cherry tree, in his *Life of General Francis Marion* (1809) has Marion offer a British officer a dinner of sweet potatoes. The officer sees that his side cannot win: "I have seen an American general and his officers, without pay, and almost without clothes, living on roots and drinking water; and all for LIBERTY! What chance have we against such men!" South Carolina artist John Blake White painted the scene in 1810; by 1840 it became a popular print and during the Civil War appeared on South Carolina currency. (Image courtesy of the Museum of Fine Arts, Boston.)

southern border with New York, plundering wayward patriots. In northern Westchester the patriot partisans, or Skinners, attacked Loyalists. The Skinners were on high alert in September 1780, as General Washington would pass north of Westchester—through West Point—to meet with General Rochambeau in Connecticut.

Lafayette had persuaded Louis XVI, after the disappointment of d'Estaing's fitful cooperation, to send a general and an army to serve under Washington's orders. It was unprecedented for a European monarch to put his officers and men under the command of a colonial rebel, but Lafayette convinced the king to send Rochambeau not to cooperate with Washington but to be deployed as Washington directed.

Washington passed through Westchester on September 20, conferred with Benedict Arnold, the commander at West Point, then moved on to meet Rochambeau. Before dawn on September 23 Washington was on his way back to New Jersey, planning to breakfast with Arnold on the Hudson.

That same morning outside Tarrytown a Skinner band—John Paulding and cousins Isaac Van Wert and David Williams—stopped a lone horseman riding south. Noticing Paulding's green and red coat—the uniform of a German sharpshooter—the stranger asked if they were "of the *upper* or *lower* party"—were they patriots or Loyalists? "Lower," they answered. Relieved, the stranger told them he was John Anderson, British officer. They ordered him off his horse. Now sensing that these were in fact patriots, he produced a pass signed by General Arnold.

Paulding ordered Anderson to strip. Out of his boots came maps and documents in the same handwriting as the signature on the pass. Of the three only Paulding could read; he saw enough to bring Anderson to their commanding officer, who ordered him taken to Arnold. Thinking better of it, he jailed Anderson, sent the documents to Washington, and sent word to Arnold that Anderson was in custody. Arnold was breakfasting with his officers when the message arrived. He told his officers he had to go to West Point, bid his wife and infant farewell, and left the house.

Washington was surprised that Arnold did not greet him when he arrived. Surprise and annoyance turned to alarm as Washington inspected West Point, the crucial link between New England and the provinces to the south. Few men were at their posts; men and guns were so scattered that West Point would be difficult to defend. Washington recrossed the Hudson to discuss the matter with Arnold.

Arnold was not home. Sitting with his officers late in the afternoon, wondering what had become of Arnold, Washington received the papers from Anderson's boot. Now he understood why West Point was so recklessly defended, though he could scarcely believe it: Arnold was a traitor.

A brilliant military commander, Arnold had been wounded at Quebec and at Saratoga. He became military governor of Philadelphia after the British left in June 1778 but lacked public administration skills and squabbled with Pennsylvania's politicians. Some Philadelphia patriots looked suspiciously on his marriage to Peggy Shippen, the beautiful daughter of a Philadelphia Loyalist merchant.

Congress, eager to drag down generals allied with Washington, investigated Arnold's administration of Philadelphia, clearing him of all but two charges—issuing an improperly documented pass and letting a citizen use a government wagon to get goods away from the British. Neither offence was serious, but Pennsylvania president Joseph Reed demanded that Arnold be court-martialed.

The court martial in January 1780 cleared Arnold of all serious charges but convicted him of these minor ones. Pennsylvania's government pressured Congress to have Washington reprimand Arnold. Congress bowed to the pressure (after all, Pennsylvania's government allowed Congress to meet in its State House), and Washington obeyed the civilian government, reluctantly writing Arnold a letter of reprimand.

This whole process rankled Arnold. His time in Philadelphia gave him little confidence in Congress, which rewarded incompetents like Gates but reprimanded him. Even before his court martial, in the spring of 1779 he began secretly corresponding with Clinton, passing information and then offering to surrender West Point for £20,000.

The first hurdle was for Arnold to be given command at West Point. Alexander Hamilton later thought Arnold's "extreme solicitude" for West Point should have "led to a suspicion of the treachery," but no one could suspect Arnold was capable of it.

Major John Andre, a British officer of Swiss descent, became Arnold's handler. He and Loyalist Beverly Robinson, whose confiscated house was Arnold's headquarters, sailed up the Hudson on September 20 to formalize plans. From the sloop *Vulture* they sent ashore two letters, one to General Israel Putnam, the other to Arnold, asking to discuss private affairs.

Washington happened to be with Arnold when the letters arrived. Arnold asked Washington what he should do. Cautious, Washington suggested not meeting with Robinson, since civilians, not soldiers, should handle private affairs.

After Washington left, Arnold brought Andre ashore under an alias—John Anderson. They spent the night and next day making plans. Clinton would move up the Hudson. Arnold would offer a brief resistance and then surrender West Point, giving Clinton what Burgoyne had failed to achieve three years earlier—British control of the Hudson. It would cut off New England and so demoralize the Americans—with the campaign going disastrously in the South—that they would come to their senses and end the war. Arnold's defection would bring other American men and officers to the British side.

Young, handsome, and urbane Major John Andre became Arnold's British handler. (Image courtesy of the Massachusetts Historical Society.)

While Arnold and Andre finalized the plan, an American officer at West Point noticed the *Vulture* in the Hudson. He prepared to bombard it, but the British sloop dropped down the river. When Andre tried to return to the *Vulture*, the American boatman refused to carry him. Arnold suggested going back to New York by land, disguised as a civilian. Andre did not like the idea, but reluctantly agreed, stuffing plans and maps in his boot, putting on civilian clothes, and riding south. On the way three Tarrytown militiamen apprehended him.

By the time Washington read the dispatches, Arnold was on the *Vulture* sailing for New York. Arnold's treason sent a momentary panic through the American staff, but they did not lose West Point or any other soldiers or officers. Washington tried to exchange Andre for Arnold, but Clinton could not give up Arnold if he wanted more American officers to desert. Andre, caught in civilian clothes, was hanged as a spy. "The discovery" of Arnold's betrayal, Greene wrote to his wife, "appears to have been providential, and convinces me that the liberties of America are the object of divine protection."

Signs of divine protection were not always easy to discern. The British held New York, Charleston, and Savannah, and the American army had

Major André, von drey America=
nern angehalten zu Tarrytown
am 23ten Septembr 1780.

In civilian clothes, Major John Andre ran into an American patrol in Westchester County, leading to the unraveling of Benedict Arnold's plot to surrender West Point. (Image courtesy of the Massachusetts Historical Society.)

collapsed in South Carolina. But in early October of 1780 South Carolina's patriot partisans defeated the Loyalists at King's Mountain, North Carolina, killing or capturing eight hundred British and Loyalist troops. Cornwallis retreated into South Carolina.

At the year's end Greene arrived to take command of what remained of the American army in the south. Like Washington, Greene understood the kind of war he had to fight. He and his men would lose a full-fledged battle with Cornwallis. But they could exhaust the British army and cut its supply lines. He would draw Cornwallis away from his supply base and through North Carolina, gradually wearing it and British public opinion down. "We fight, get beat, rise, and fight again," he wrote. In January 1781 Marion's men beat Tarleton's regiment at Cowpens in South Carolina, capturing nine hundred British and Loyalist troops. Defeating the dreaded Tarleton bolstered the Americans' spirit.

Clinton's strategy was to pacify South Carolina and Georgia, empowering the local Loyalists to keep down the patriots. Cornwallis believed Virginia was the source of supplies for Greene and the patriot militias. A strike at Virginia, he thought, could end the war; at least British control of the Chesapeake would end the rebellion in North Carolina, Maryland, and Virginia.

Against Clinton's wishes, and even without his knowledge, Cornwallis moved toward Virginia. Arnold raided Virginia at the end of 1780, attacking Richmond and driving the state government to Charlottesville, where the British nearly captured Governor Jefferson. Washington sent Lafayette to protect Virginia.

As Cornwallis moved toward Virginia, Greene moved south to challenge him. The two armies met at Guilford Courthouse in Greensboro, North Carolina. Cornwallis won the battle but suffered heavy casualties. He was too far inland from his supply lines, and local Loyalists did not rise up in the wake of the British victory. "The idea of our friends rising in numbers, and to any purpose, totally failed," the victorious Cornwallis wrote to Clinton. The victory left him no choice but to retreat back to Wilmington, near the coast, abandoning the conquered territory. He marched north again in May 1781 to join Arnold in Virginia. "I assure you," he wrote Clinton, "that I am quite tired of marching about the country in quest of adventures."

Weary, Cornwallis established a Chesapeake base at Yorktown. With the British army in Virginia, Greene penned up the British in Charleston, and, with the aid of South Carolina's partisan bands, took their back-country posts one by one.

With a war of attrition being fought in the South, Washington and Rochambeau met to devise a strategy in 1781. They knew their actions required French sea power, and that Admiral François-Joseph Paul, Comte de Grasse, sailing from France to Haiti in March, would cooperate only on his way to or from the Caribbean. With the American war a stale-mate, both England and France were concentrating on the West Indies, where the French had taken Tobago, Saint Vincent, Dominica, and Saint Christopher from the British, who had themselves taken Montserrat and Nevis from the French. Spanish forces from New Orleans had taken the British posts at Pensacola and Mobile, garrisoned with British regulars, Pennsylvania Loyalists, Indians, and Germans.

Washington and Rochambeau hoped Admiral de Grasse could pre-vent Cornwallis's reinforcement by attacking New York, or at least keep-ing the British fleet in port. They learned in midsummer that de Grasse, with twenty-eight ships and three thousand French and Haitian soldiers, was bound for the Chesapeake. Washington saw an opportunity. He called for more New England militia and ordered Rochambeau's army—except for "ten of Soissonais who had gone back to their sweethearts at Newport"—from Rhode Island to White Plains. Washington prepared another ruse—giving the appearance of preparing to besiege New York, by fortifying the Palisades and building bakery ovens in New Jersey—while sending his men to Virginia. Clinton, meanwhile, saw that the French had left Rhode Island, so his forces took Newport.

By this time de Grasse had disembarked three thousand men and artil-lery pieces around Yorktown and ferried Washington's men down the Chesapeake. A small British naval force skirmished unsuccessfully with de Grasse, then returned to New York. Most of the British fleet stayed in the West Indies, to which de Grasse returned in early September.

Cornwallis saw now that he held, in his words, "a defensive post which cannot have the smallest influence on the war in Carolina, and which only gives us some acres of unhealthy swamp, and is forever liable to become a prey to a foreign enemy with a temporary superiority at sea." He thought he was surrounded by twenty thousand French and American soldiers. Though Washington and Rochambeau had only sixteen thousand, they still far outnumbered Cornwallis's seven thousand men, and kept them under heavy artillery bombardment. Cornwallis tried to escape across the

Landung einer Französischen Hülfs. Armee in America, zu Rhode Island. am 11 ten Julius 1780.

The arrival of French forces under General Rochambeau changed the nature of the war. (Image courtesy of the Massachusetts Historical Society.)

York River, but by mid-October he realized reinforcements would not come. Like Burgoyne at Saratoga, he had no choice but surrender.

Too ill to attend the surrender ceremony, Cornwallis sent General Charles O'Hara. On horseback, General O'Hara approached the allied officers with great dignity. He first offered his sword to Rochambeau. It was less humiliating to surrender to a European officer than to an American provincial. But Rochambeau corrected him. He was "only auxiliary," Rochambeau said. "The American General must receive the orders." O'Hara approached Washington.

Realizing that O'Hara was not Cornwallis, but his second, Washington directed O'Hara to his own second, Benjamin Lincoln. Since taking command of this army six years earlier, Washington had been irked by British refusal to recognize his rank. He returned unopened letters from the British officers addressed to "Mr. Washington" or "Colonel Washington," not merely because he was sensitive to his own rank, but because he was sensitive to his country's. He would refuse to deal with the British unless they recognized the sovereignty of the United States.

O'Hara presented Lincoln his sword; Lincoln returned it, and the British soldiers marched through the lines of Americans and French to lay down their own weapons. They turned their faces toward the French, attempting to ignore the Americans. Lafayette, commanding American troops, had his band strike up "Yankee Doodle." Angered at this insult, added to their injured pride, some British soldiers smashed their weapons as they lay them down.

London did not blame Cornwallis but Lord North and the British ministry, which had won the Parliamentary elections of 1780. News of the surrender, of de Grasse's victory at St. Kitts, and of the Spanish capture of Minorca turned the public mood. Opposition-leader Henry Conway, who had introduced the Stamp Act, moved to end the American war. This motion passed over the king's opposition. North, as he had done every year, submitted his resignation; this time the king accepted it.

British emissaries now met in France with Franklin, John Adams, and Henry Laurens (who had been captured at sea by the British and exchanged for Cornwallis) to work out a peace treaty. While British forces still held New York and Charleston, Clinton suspended military operations; Washington would not disband his army as long as the British army remained in America.

Keeping the army together was Washington's greatest triumph. Over the course of the war, 230,000 men served in the Continental Army, with another 145,000 serving in state militias; many served multiple enlistments, so in total perhaps 250,000 men bore arms on the American side from 1775 to 1783. It is difficult, if not impossible, to determine exactly how many served; it is even more difficult to determine why they did so. Anecdotes and pension records reveal only part of the story.

One of the Revolution's first historians, Peter Oliver, had a unique vantage point: he was a Tory, former chief justice of Massachusetts, sent into exile when the British evacuated Boston in 1776. After Bunker Hill, Oliver interviewed a wounded American lieutenant, William Scott of Peterborough, New Hampshire. Why was Scott fighting? According to Oliver's account, Scott saw his neighbors getting commissions, and he refused to enlist as a private but would serve as an officer. He joined in order to better his life: "As to the Dispute between great Britain & the Colonies, I know nothing of it; neither am I capable of judging whether it is right or wrong."

Oliver regarded Scott's motives as typical for the rebels. Historian John Shy has shown that ambition and perhaps jealousy motivated Scott to seek a commission. But ambition and jealousy alone do not explain why, after Scott had been taken as a prisoner to Halifax, he escaped and made his way to join the defense of New York in 1776. He escaped again after the fall of Fort Washington by swimming across the Hudson; back in New Hampshire he raised his own company, which included two of his sons, the elder of whom died of camp fever after six years in the army. Over the course of the war Scott lost his son, his wife, his farm, and his property.

What made men like Scott serve? In Scott's town, every adult male served at some point in the war. A third of the men, like Scott, stayed on for more than a year. Scott became an officer; most remained privates. Who were they? Studies of Peterborough and other towns reveal that this hard core of soldiers consisted of men who had few other options for employment. A signing bonus on enlistment, or the offer of a grant of land after the war, was an inducement to join or to stay in the service.

Wives or sisters of the soldiers would often accompany the army, serving as nurses, cooks, and menders of uniforms. Though Washington objected to having so many women with his army and tried to resist women's demands for rations, he recognized the limits of his authority. His own wife, Martha, was with him during most of the war, so he could hardly object to the wives of enlisted men staying in camp. Washington objected to women riding in the wagons when the army moved, but he discovered he could not prevent it.

Women at home made uniforms and blankets for the troops, and women who sold produce or clothing could also act as spies, entering British camps or entertaining British officers who occupied the cities. The women of Philadelphia went door to door in 1779, so persistently, one Loyalist woman wrote, that "people were obliged to give them something to get rid of them." Their persistence paid off, as they raised over $300,000 for the soldiers. Washington wanted to put their contribution in his general fund; the women wanted to make a direct gift of two dollars, hard money, to each soldier. Washington refused, fearing the men would buy drinks; the Philadelphia women instead gave a shirt to each soldier.

Deborah Samson of Massachusetts is both representative of the soldier's experience and a complete aberration. Her father abandoned the family—Deborah's mother and seven children—when Deborah was six; she was bound out to a neighboring farm, where she grew tall and strong working in the fields. She taught herself to read and write by reviewing schoolwork of the boys in the family, and when she was eighteen, in 1778, she became a schoolteacher. In May of 1782 she enlisted in a Massachusetts regiment under the name Robert Shurtliff, received sixty pounds as an enlistment bonus, and was marched to West Point to keep the British isolated in New York. During a skirmish near Tarrytown she was cut in the head by a British saber, and shot in the thigh by a musket. A doctor treated the saber cut, but she did not mention the musket ball in her leg, cutting it out herself. When her unit went to Philadelphia, she became ill, was treated by a doctor who discovered her gender, and was given an honorable discharge; later, Massachusetts awarded her a pension.

As Robert Shurtliff, her story is representative of the soldier's experience in the war; as Deborah Samson, she was unique. While women supported the army, they did not serve; and those women who did as cooks, nurses, or in other roles, did not receive pay or pensions. In 1832, after years of petitioning from widows of soldiers, Congress awarded pensions to enlisted men's widows, a first. But nearly fifty years after the war ended, few widows were left to collect.

Pensions were far in the future; Washington had the more immediate problem of keeping his men fed, clothed, trained, and together. Three-year enlistments began to expire in 1780; men who had not been paid in months began deserting individually or mutinying collectively. One hundred Massachusetts men marched out of West Point in January 1780; some were brought back and punished, others pardoned. Connecticut troops marched out of Morristown in May. The following month thirty-one New Yorkers deserted Fort Stanwix; their commander, along with Oneida allies, pursued and shot thirteen of them.

Fifteen hundred of the twenty-five hundred Pennsylvania troops marched out of Morristown to Princeton in January 1781, occupying the college buildings to demand that Congress let them go home—they had served three years (though they had enlisted for three years or the war's duration); they also wanted their pay. They told their commander, General Anthony Wayne, that their grievance was not with him but with Congress. Congress sent an emissary, Pennsylvania president Joseph Reed. General Henry Clinton also sent emissaries to offer the mutineers British protection. The mutineers sent the British agents to Wayne as prisoners. Their object was not treason but pay. Reed and Wayne agreed to release men whose terms were up.

New Jersey troops mutinied later that month. Washington arrived to put the mutiny down by force, having a firing squad of pardoned mutineers shoot two ringleaders. Washington knew mutinies had to be suppressed, but he also knew mutinies were an inevitable consequence of "keeping an army without pay, cloathing, and (frequently without provision)."

Congress seemed unable to resolve the problem; debts mounted and Continental currency became worthless. Washington would not disband his army until the British army had left; the officers and men were reluctant to leave until they had been paid. A delegation of officers went to Congress in January 1783, demanding their promised pensions (half-pay for life, granted in October 1780 as an inducement to stay in service). Colonel Walter Stewart returned to headquarters at Newburgh, New York with alarming news: Congress was considering disbanding the army without honoring the pensions. An aide to Horatio Gates drafted a call to the officers to use their power to force Congress to pay or to replace Congress with an effective government that could pay them. Was this a call for a military coup? Certainly the armed officers had more power than the ineffectual Congress.

Where did Washington stand? He ordered his officers to cancel their planned meeting and called another on March 15, 1783. Washington denounced threats to subvert civil authority, pledged his own efforts to secure his officers' pay, and concluded, "Let me entreat you, gentlemen, on your part, not to take any measures which, viewed in the calm light of reason, will lessen the dignity and sully the glory you have hitherto maintained; let me request you to rely on the plighted faith of your country, and place a full confidence in the purity of the intentions of Congress."

"You will, by the dignity of your conduct, afford occasion for posterity to say, when speaking of the glorious example you have exhibited to mankind, 'had this day been wanting, the world had never seen the last stage of perfection to which human nature is capable of attaining.'"

Not sure he had convinced them, Washington pulled a letter from his pocket; Congressman Joseph Jones outlined to Washington the steps Congress was taking to pay the officers. Washington could not read Jones's handwriting. He reached again into his pocket and this time drew out a pair of glasses. The officers were stunned. None had ever seen Washington wear glasses. He put on the glasses, looking at the assembled silent men. "Gentlemen," he said, "you must pardon me. I have grown gray in your service and now find myself growing blind."

He finished and left, and the officers rejected any attempt to subvert civil authority. Washington had prevented a military coup.

But this did not resolve the problem. In June several hundred Pennsylvania soldiers marched on Philadelphia and surrounded the state house, giving the men inside—Congress and the Pennsylvania Assembly—twenty minutes to pay them or face the consequences. Though they managed to appease the soldiers, the members of Congress felt insulted, feared further attacks from the soldiers they could not pay, and resented the Pennsylvania government's unwillingness to protect them (Congress had wanted Pennsylvania to have its militia drive off the Continental soldiers). Congress left Philadelphia. Six years earlier Congress had fled Philadelphia to escape the British army; now it fled from its own. John Armstrong wrote, "The grand Sanhedrin of the Nation, with all their solemnity and emptiness, have removed to Princeton and left a state where their wisdom has been long questioned, their virtue suspected, and their dignity a jest."

Who would take power? In London, King George III asked the American-born artist Benjamin West what Washington would do now that he and his army had won the war. To the king it seemed obvious that Washington would use his army to form a government. West predicted

Washington would now go back home to his farm. "If he does that," the king replied, "he will be the greatest man in the world."

Washington knew a stronger union was essential to sustain independence and pay off the significant debt. He also knew its strength had to be achieved politically, not militarily. He wrote to the governors of the states, urging them to foster a stronger union. When he learned in October that the peace treaty was signed and that Clinton was preparing to evacuate New York, he disbanded his own army and prepared to enter the last remaining British outpost in what was now the independent United States.

On November 20 he reached the Harlem River and, with Governor George Clinton at his side, crossed over into Manhattan, seven years after he and his army had been driven from it. As the British prepared to sail from Staten Island, Washington and his men marched down Broadway. A New York woman contrasted the two armies:

> We had been accustomed for a long time to military display in all the finish and finery of garrison life; the troops just leaving us were as if equipped for show, and with their scarlet uniforms and burnished arms, made a brilliant display; the troops that marched in, on the contrary, were ill-clad and weather beaten, and made a forlorn appearance; but then they were *our* troops, and as I looked at them and thought upon all they had done and suffered for us, my heart and my eyes were full, and I admired and gloried in them the more, because they were weather beaten and forlorn.

Washington bid his officers farewell on December 4, then made his way to Annapolis, where Congress was in session. He returned his commission, retiring, as he said, from the great theater of action, and continued home to Mount Vernon. The war was over. Independence had been achieved. But could the new nation create a government that would sustain independence, preserve individual liberty, and allow it to repay its debts? The possibility of doing this seemed as remote in 1783 as the prospect of independence had in 1776.

CHAPTER 5

WAS AMERICA DIFFERENT?

THOMAS PAINE HAD BOLDLY TOLD THE AMERICANS THAT THEY
had it in their power to start the world anew. Would they? How would
their new country be different from every other nation in the world?

Even before the revolution, visitors from Europe commented on the
striking differences between the old world and the new, such as America's
physical landscape, the population's high rate of literacy, and the institution of slavery. After the Revolution, these features continued to set
America apart, but so did two other differences that developed in the
years of Revolution: religious diversity and government institutions.

Every American state except Pennsylvania and Rhode Island had an
established church, but religious practices differed in each. Tremendous
immigration from Northern Ireland, Scotland, and Germany in the
mid-eighteenth century brought dissenting Presbyterians, Moravians,
Lutherans, and Baptists, but not their clergy. American believers created
their own communities of worship and controlled them in ways they
could not have in Europe, where every community had an established,
tax-supported church, and where priests and bishops were often political
appointees. In America, children of one faith met and married children
of another. Religious diversity, which did not exist anywhere else, flour-
ished in America.

American Baptists presented the biggest challenge to religious ortho-
doxy. Reverend Isaac Backus of Massachusetts appeared uninvited at the
first Continental Congress in 1774, bringing copies of his *Appeal to the
Public for Religious Liberty*. He complained that the Massachusetts assembly taxed his Baptist congregation to support the Congregational clergy—
a violation of their "No taxation without representation" principle.

Congress pushed the Massachusetts delegates—the Adamses, Hancock, and Robert Treat Paine—to meet with Backus, but the four-hour discussion accomplished little. Robert Treat Paine thought that "there was nothing of conscience in the matter; it was only a contending about paying a little money." This was just what Parliament said about the Stamp and Tea Acts. For the Baptists it was about more than a little money: they denied the state's power to interfere in matters of religious conscience.

Emboldened by Congress's support, Backus petitioned the Massachusetts Provincial Congress for relief. Some Congregationalists suspected the Baptists were in cahoots with Anglicans in support of British rule, and the Provincial Congress would have ignored Backus but for John Adams insisting that they needed to act or risk the support of non-Congregationalists in other states. The Provincial Congress did not exactly take action— it told the Baptists to petition their assembly when it met again.

Baptists in Virginia suffered more than unfair taxation: the established church could have them arrested for not attending Anglican services. The Baptists protested, and though Virginia's 1776 Constitution guaranteed freedom of conscience, state taxes continued to support the Episcopal clergy. The Baptists protested, threatening to withhold support from the Revolutionary cause. They found powerful allies in Thomas Jefferson and young James Madison, an Episcopalian who had studied under Presbyterian elder John Witherspoon at Princeton. When Jefferson revised Virginia's legal code in the 1770s, he proposed a statute for religious freedom, declaring that

> no man shall be compelled to frequent or support any religious worship, place, or ministry whatsoever, nor shall be enforced, restrained, molested, or burdened in his body or goods, nor shall otherwise suffer on account of his religious opinions or beliefs, but that all men shall be free to profess, and by argument to maintain their opinions in matters of religion, and that the same shall in no wise diminish, enlarge, or affect their civil capacities.

The legislature rejected the measure, but Madison continued to press it. Finally in 1785 he won the passage of this statute, freeing Baptists and others from an Episcopalian establishment and from having to pay taxes to support a church to which they did not belong. Jefferson wrote that this law guaranteed religious liberty to "the Jew and the Gentile, the Christian and the Mahometan, the Hindoo, and infidel of every denomination."

The fact that Virginia's government had continued to tax Baptists, Jews, Muslims, Hindus, and infidels to support the Episcopalians, despite a constitutional guarantee of religious toleration, made Madison wary of "parchment barriers" to defend minorities against majorities. It also showed him a solution to the dilemma of governing the newly independent United States. In each state a majority could form on local issues, with little to check its will. Virginia Episcopalians, or Massachusetts Congregationalists, could tax Baptists and other religious dissenters who would never form a local majority.

But, Madison realized, while one religious sect could wield power in a single state, the United States encompassed so many different religious sects that it would be impossible for one to dominate nationally. This very diversity of religious practices secured religious liberty across the United States. With so many different churches, there could be no single established church. Madison saw that religious diversity, or pluralism, would prevent a national religious establishment. He also saw this as a model for preventing other forms—economic or political—of majority tyranny. The nation as a whole would encompass so many people with different interests—cultural, political, and economic—that no single interest was likely to form a majority to tyrannize over minority interests.

It was apparent that the loosely constructed confederation of thirteen autonomous states was not working. The United States could not pay its debts—it defaulted on its loan from France in 1785; it could not protect its frontiers—the British kept their forts in the Ohio territory, arming the Native Americans to attack frontier settlements, while Spain refused to allow Americans to use the Mississippi River; and it could not protect its merchants—Algiers in 1785 captured two American ships and held the sailors hostage.

But how to reform the system? James Madison realized the confederation had to give way to a government resting directly on the people. He prepared a memorandum listing the confederation's problems. All centered on one point: the states had too much power. Their governments could change laws capriciously, making laws complicated and confusing. Any one state could block reform in Congress, making it unable to pay debts or enforce treaties. But because the states' legislatures, not the people, elected Congress, it could not tax citizens or use military force against them.

In the summer of 1787, the states (all but Rhode Island, which saw no reason to change the system) sent delegates to a convention in

Philadelphia. Madison and the Virginia delegates took the lead, arriving at the convention first. Along with Madison, Virginia sent Washington; Governor Edmund Randolph; George Mason, author of the state constitution; and George Wythe, the leading law teacher in the United States (he had trained Jefferson and John Marshall). From Pennsylvania came James Wilson, a Scotland-trained lawyer, and two unrelated Morrises: Robert, minister of finance, and Gouverneur, the younger son of a New York aristocrat. Former governor John Rutledge; General Charles Cotesworth Pinckney, wartime aide to Washington; and Charles Pinckney, an opinionated young lawyer, came from South Carolina. Other delegates included John Dickinson, author of the series of essays known as *Letters from a Farmer in Pennsylvania* and drafter of the Articles of Confederation; the chief justices of New York and New Jersey; the president of Columbia College; Maryland lawyer Luther Martin; and Elbridge Gerry and Rufus King from Massachusetts.

Jefferson called it an assembly of "demigods," but he was not there, nor were other important Americans. Patrick Henry stayed away, as did Governor George Clinton of New York; Governor John Hancock and Samuel Adams of Massachusetts, Minister of Foreign Affairs John Jay, and Jefferson's fellow diplomat John Adams were absent. Nor were there any representatives from Rhode Island, or from west of the Appalachians; all the delegates were men, all were white, and only three had what might be considered "common origins": Franklin, the son of a soap maker, now one of the wealthiest men in the country; Alexander Hamilton, born to an unwed mother in the West Indies; and former cobbler Roger Sherman.

Virginia's governor, Randolph, proposed a plan Madison had drafted to create a national government with a national legislature, executive, and judiciary. The two-house legislature, elected by the people, would be able to veto state laws and tax people in the states. Representation in both legislative houses would be based on population; Virginia wanted to end the system that gave Delaware or Rhode Island as much power as Virginia or Pennsylvania.

Leaders from the smaller states would not give their power to larger states and knew the American people would not either. Dickinson pointedly told the nationalists they had pushed the matter too far—though the delegates might prefer a national government, the people would never ratify it. The small-state leaders drafted their own plan to strengthen the confederation by giving the existing Congress power to tax citizens, and by making the new Constitution "the supreme law of the land," binding all state officials—including judges—to follow federal, not state law. But the nationalists would not budge. They wanted population to count in both legislative houses.

With the convention threatening to dissolve, Sherman and William Samuel Johnson, both from Connecticut, proposed a compromise: one house of the legislature would represent states in proportion to their population, and in the other each state would be equally represented. The nationalists opposed it, but a committee adopted the proposal, saving the Constitution and opening the way to discuss other issues.

Gouverneur Morris proposed restricting the right to vote to freeholders—individuals who owned property. In response to the objection that restricting voting rights would lead to an aristocracy, Morris said that he "had long learned not to be the dupe of words" such as *aristocracy.* "Give the votes to people who have no property, and they will sell them to the rich who will be able to buy them." He warned that in the future "this country will abound with mechanics & manufacturers who will receive their bread from their employers." Would these hirelings be "secure & faithful Guardians of liberty? Will they be the impregnable barrier against aristocracy?" Most people in 1787 were freeholders; they would not object. Urban merchants could buy land "if they have wealth and value the right" to vote. "If not they don't deserve it."

John Dickinson also thought freeholders were "the best guardians of liberty." Restricting the vote to them would guard against the "dangerous influence of those multitudes without property & without principle" who would one day abound. Men who owned their own land were independent; their employees were not. "The great mass of our Citizens is composed at this time of freeholders, and will be pleased with it."

Madison worried about "the probable reception" Morris's change "would meet with in the States" where nonfreeholders could vote. Passing the Constitution would be difficult enough without creating unnecessary obstacles. On the other hand, freeholders were the safest guardians of liberty, and in the future the "great majority of the people will not only be without landed, but any other sort of, property." If the propertyless joined together neither liberty nor property would be safe; more likely they would simply "become the tools of opulence & ambition."

Oliver Ellsworth of Connecticut warned that "the right of suffrage was a tender point," and people would not support a constitution that took it away. Pierce Butler of South Carolina agreed. George Mason, author of Virginia's constitution, owner of much land and several hundred slaves, rose to defend the propertyless. Every "man having evidence of attachment to & permanent common interest with the Society ought to share in all its rights & privileges." Merchants and capitalists had an attachment, but Mason went further. "Ought the merchant, the monied man, the parent of a number of children whose fortunes are to be pursued in his own Country, to be viewed as suspicious characters, and unworthy to be trusted with the common right of their fellow Citizen?" Mason looked to the future and saw large propertyless families not as threats to liberty and property but instead as full of children who would pursue their fortunes in their own country.

Benjamin Franklin knew what Mason meant. His parents owned no property but raised seven children and thirteen grandchildren respectably. Franklin, usually quiet in legislative bodies, had only spoken a dozen times thus far, asking a question or making a comment to illuminate the discussion. Twice he gave long speeches, writing them out in advance and sitting quietly, sagelike, as another delegate read his words. This time he did not need to write down his speech.

"It is of great consequence that we should not depress the virtue & public spirit of our common people," Franklin began. This was not the sage who had charmed Louis XVI, nor was he speaking as one of the wealthiest men in the country. Franklin spoke as the son of a Boston soap maker, reminding the other delegates that the common people had "displayed a great deal" of virtue and public spirit "during the war," and they had "contributed principally to the favorable issue of it." American sailors, on the lowest rung of the economic ladder, preferred when captured at sea to stay in horrible British prisons rather than serve on British warships. He contrasted "their patriotism" with the British sailors who eagerly joined the American fleet. Why was this? It was because common people were treated differently in America and in Britain. Franklin had been a poor man in both countries, and knew the difference. He recalled an episode of British history when a timid Parliament suppressed dangerous "tumultuous meetings" by restricting the vote to freeholders; the next year a more confident Parliament subjected "the people who had no votes to peculiar labors and hardships." The convention decided not to go down the path of England.

How to choose the executive proved only slightly less difficult. Should he be chosen by the Congress? By the state legislatures? By the people as a whole? Would citizens of Georgia know of possible candidates in Massachusetts, and vice versa? Could foreign nations influence the election through bribery? Morris created an elaborate system for choosing a president, taking into account the country's size and regional differences. Each state would choose electors—who did not hold any other office—having the same number as its representatives in Congress, including senators. These electors would gather in their state capitals on the same day, every four years, and vote for two people— only one of whom could be from their own state. They would send all of these sealed votes to Congress, which would count them. Morris and the delegates assumed that no one would receive a majority, but that some candidates would have support in different regions. The House of Representatives would choose from the top five candidates, with each state having one vote.

The candidate receiving the most votes would be president. The runner-up would become vice president, taking office in case of the president's incapacity, but his main role would be to preside over the Senate.

It was an elaborate system, which assumed the electors would be a nominating board; the House of Representatives would make the final choice. The states would have an important role. Only once, in 1824, did the system work as the framers imagined it would. That year four candidates split the electoral vote, and Congress elected John Quincy Adams. Before then, in the 1790s, national political parties developed that arranged the electors' votes in advance.

The convention voted to give Congress the power to regulate interstate and international commerce. But should Congress have the power to tax imports? This power in Parliament's hands had caused the Revolution. George Mason recognized that Virginia depended on international markets for its tobacco. He would not want Europeans to close their tobacco markets in retaliation for American tariffs on European manufactured goods. He proposed requiring a two-thirds vote of Congress to impose tariffs. The manufacturing states—Pennsylvania and New England—would support higher protective tariffs and would probably come to have majorities in Congress, but the two-thirds vote would protect the agricultural states.

Mason also joined Luther Martin of Maryland in calling for Congress to end the slave trade. At this moment in England, a public campaign was being waged against the horrors of the slave trade, which the British dominated. It is not surprising that Americans took up the cause, though it is a bit jarring that slave-owners Mason and Martin made the case against the slave trade. Mason, owner of more than two hundred slaves, wanted the Constitution to take a stand against this barbaric traffic. "Every master of slaves is born a petty tyrant," Mason warned, and slavery would "bring the judgment of heaven on a Country." Slavery itself weakened a society and depressed the value of free labor. Looking westward, he noted that the settlers in the new territories across the mountains were "already calling out for slaves for their new lands."

Connecticut's Oliver Ellsworth "had never owned a slave" and so "could not judge the effects of slavery on character," but he advised against raising so divisive an issue. If slavery were as evil as Mason said, then Ellsworth thought they should "go farther and free those already in the Country," but if they would not do that, restricting the slave trade would be unfair to South Carolina and Georgia, which still needed slaves to work in their massive agricultural industry. South Carolina's Pinckneys, and Luther Baldwin of Georgia, warned that their states would reject the Constitution if it barred their importing slaves. They also said the Virginians and Marylanders were not humanitarians—they were not calling for an end to slavery but only the importation of more slaves from Africa. The Virginians had more slaves than were needed on the exhausted tobacco fields and wanted to sell their surplus slaves to South Carolina and Georgia. By barring imports from Africa, the Virginians were not advancing the cause of humanity but only the value of Virginia's surplus slave population.

The convention sent both issues—slave trade and tariff—to a committee. New Englanders, neutral on the slave trade but against the two-thirds vote on tariffs, made a bargain with Georgians and South Carolinians, who wanted the two-thirds tariff vote and to continue the slave trade. Georgia and South Carolina would support a simple majority vote on tariffs, and in return they could continue importing slaves for twenty years.

Outraged at this bargain, George Mason said he would sooner cut off his right hand than use it to sign the Constitution. Still, in an effort to save the Constitution, Mason and Elbridge Gerry proposed a bill of rights. Mason said most state constitutions began with bills of rights, listing the rights the government could not violate. The people would expect one in this constitution. But the other delegates pleaded weariness and rejected the call to draft a bill of rights. Mason and Gerry refused to sign the Constitution. Mason, according to James Madison, "left Philadelphia in a very ill humor indeed," while Gerry warned of a civil war brewing in Massachusetts between proponents of democracy, which he called "the worst of all political evils," and their equally violent adversaries. Gerry feared this constitution would not calm but would further agitate the political waters. Despite their opposition, the convention submitted the Constitution to Congress, which sent it to the states, nine of which would have to ratify it in order for it to take effect.

Quickly supporters mobilized. Philadelphia writer Pelatiah Webster endorsed the Constitution in a pamphlet proclaiming it "federal," as opposed to "national." Supporters of the Constitution thus became Federalists. James Wilson argued that a bill of rights would be dangerous and unnecessary, as the new government had limited powers, and any powers not specifically granted were reserved to the people or to the states. Where in this Constitution was there any power over the press, religion, or speech? Where did it say anything about jury trials, or about the rights of criminal defendants, or the right to keep and bear arms? Wilson argued that if the Constitution included a bill of rights, it would imply the federal government had powers in these areas—press, religion, speech, rights of the accused—when in fact only the states did, and the state bills of rights would continue to protect citizens in the states.

Opponents emerged just as quickly, objecting that the new government had too much power, that it would overwhelm the state governments, and that the Constitution lacked a bill of rights. "I confess, as I enter the building I stumble at the threshold," Samuel Adams wrote to Richard Henry Lee. "I meet with a national government, instead of a confederation of states." The very preamble—"We, the People of the United States" —asserted that this government rested on the people of the nation, obliterating state boundaries. Article VI, Section 2, says that the Constitution and the laws made under it are the "supreme Law of the Land," and all state judges were bound to follow federal precedent, "any Thing in the Constitution or Laws of any State to the Contrary notwithstanding." Did this not make state bills of rights irrelevant?

As for Wilson's argument that the federal government had no power over things bills of rights protected, opponents pointed to Article I, Section 9, which says that the right of habeas corpus cannot be suspended. If this right—to have charges formally filed within twenty-four hours of being arrested, so an accused person cannot simply be held—could not be suspended, did that mean other rights could? Did the federal government have other power over judicial proceedings? And while Article I, Section 8 specifically listed Congress's powers, it began and ended with two ominous grants of power: Congress would have the power to "pay the Debts and provide for the common Defence and...general Welfare of the United States," and Congress would have power to "make all laws which shall be necessary and proper for carrying into Execution the foregoing Powers." Patrick Henry called this the "sweeping clause," which would sweep away all state powers.

Delaware and New Jersey quickly and unanimously ratified the Constitution. Georgia also supported the Constitution, needing the new government's help in its war against the Creeks. Pennsylvania's ratifying convention met in December, and though the opposition had mobilized, protesting the lack of a bill of rights and the new government's powers, they were outvoted. In the first month of 1788, conventions met in Connecticut, New Hampshire, and Massachusetts. The first two states were expected to ratify easily, if not unanimously. Connecticut did, but New Hampshire's Federalists realized when the convention assembled that their opponents outnumbered them, and adjourned.

Massachusetts posed a problem for the Federalists. Samuel Adams opposed the Constitution; John Hancock was keeping quiet; and the convention elected in the fall of 1787 included about eighteen or twenty delegates who had been in arms at the beginning of the year opposing the powers of the state government. This convention was unlikely to support a more powerful federal government. The Massachusetts Federalists prepared a compromise. If Massachusetts would first ratify, they would draw up amendments to add when the Constitution took effect. The Federalists drew up a list of amendments they could accept, and by a vote of 187 to 168 Massachusetts ratified, pledging to propose amendments once the new government formed.

Subsequently, South Carolina and Maryland ratified, each proposing amendments. Charles Cotesworth Pinckney had addressed the demand for a bill of rights in the South Carolina convention, pointing out that bills of rights generally began by declaring that "all men are born free and equal." "We should make such an assertion with a very ill grace," he said, "since most of our people are actually born slaves."

Eight states now had ratified. Rhode Island rejected the Constitution by a popular vote, and North Carolina's convention was also certain to reject it. New Hampshire, New York, and Virginia were all in doubt when their conventions met in June. James Madison faced off in Virginia's convention against Patrick Henry, a brilliant orator and a formidable power in state government. Henry warned of the dangers to liberty if the Constitution were ratified. Henry charged that the Constitution would sacrifice religious liberty; Madison reminded the delegates that the Virginia Constitution promised religious liberty, but until the state passed the statute for religious freedom, Baptists and other dissenters were taxed to support the Episcopal Church. He did not need to remind them that he had been the prime mover in passing the Virginia statute; Henry had been its chief opponent. And while George Mason blasted the Constitution for allowing the slave trade to continue, Henry attacked it for threatening the institution of slavery.

Madison proved more convincing and ultimately agreed that amendments could be added after ratification. By a vote of eighty-nine to seventy-nine, Virginia ratified and offered forty amendments to be added later. By this time New Hampshire had become the ninth state to ratify. When the New York convention learned that the Constitution would take effect, it ratified as well.

The new government elected under the Constitution met in New York in the spring of 1789. The electors unanimously chose Washington to be the first president of the United States. John Adams, with thirty-four votes, was elected vice president. Most states sent supporters of the Constitution to the Senate. In House elections there were a few surprises. Fisher Ames defeated Samuel Adams in Boston; in Virginia, Madison defeated James Monroe, the ratification opponent.

After creating a Department of State to oversee foreign affairs, a Treasury, a Department of War, the office of attorney general, a five-member Supreme Court, and district courts in each state, Congress turned its attention to drafting a bill of rights. Madison had opposed adding amendments but now saw them as the price of ratification. He took the proposals submitted by the states, as well as the state declarations of rights, and from this multitude of proposals drafted twelve articles of amendment for submission to the states.

Washington appointed able men to the new positions in the federal government. John Jay, the minister for foreign affairs, became chief justice, but also acted as secretary of state until Thomas Jefferson accepted the position. Alexander Hamilton became secretary of the treasury. Henry Knox, minister of war, became secretary of war, and Virginia governor Edmund Randolph became attorney general. Washington anticipated harmony, but political divisions soon emerged, over both domestic policy and international affairs.

The clearest division emerged in America in reaction to the revolution in France. The French people in 1789 overthrew the government, which could not cope with the great divide between rich and poor or find an equitable way to pay France's tremendous debt. Americans welcomed the spread of the cause of liberty—Jefferson, the American minister to France, watched with approval as the French assembly demanded more power; Lafayette called for a constitutional monarchy, and Thomas Paine was elected to the French assembly and wrote its manifesto, *A Vindication of the Rights of Man*. But the revolution devolved into anarchy, with more radical factions calling for the elimination of aristocracy, the church, and all vestiges of the old order.

Vice President John Adams warned that France was headed for trouble. No country could simply toss out its old government without risking chaos. A Philadelphia mob stormed the newspaper that printed Adams's musings, charging that Adams admired aristocracy and monarchy. Across the country, citizens supporting France formed "Democratic Republican Societies," modeled on France's Jacobin clubs, celebrating the French Revolution as an aftereffect of the American Revolution and embracing the cause of liberty, equality, and fraternity.

As Americans divided over France, treasury secretary Hamilton proposed that the United States pay the states' Revolutionary War debts, impose an excise tax on whiskey to help pay this debt, and create a national bank to help the government borrow money. Madison opposed these policies, arguing first that Virginia and other states had already paid their debts and that their citizens should not have to pay the debts of others; that paying the debt in this way would not help the soldiers who had served but only those speculators who had bought up the debt; that an excise tax was politically unwise; and that a national bank violated the Constitution, since Congress did not have the power to charter corporations.

Hamilton argued that the war debt had been incurred for the nation's benefit. He believed that it was essential to secure the support of capitalists and speculators; that an excise tax on whiskey, though politically unpopular, was necessary and would bring revenues from the frontier; and that while the Constitution did not give Congress power to charter a bank, it did not forbid it to do so. This and other powers not specifically granted were implied by the "necessary and proper" clause.

Political parties developed along these fault lines. The Democratic-Republicans, led by Madison and Jefferson, generally opposed the Washington administration's policies, while the Federalists, led by Alexander Hamilton, supported them. Washington remained enough of a national icon to be above party politics, and the Federalists did not think of themselves as a party but as the government of the United States. Their strength was in New England and among the merchants of Philadelphia, the Virginia tidewater gentry, and the South Carolina rice planters. The Republicans, as the opposition came to be called, drew strength from the frontier, from urban artisans and smaller traders, from New York farmers and the supporters of Pennsylvania's radical constitution, and from the piedmont and backcountry of Virginia and the Carolinas. These political divisions played out against the backdrop of the French Revolution. The Republicans charged that Federalists were trying to impose monarchy or aristocracy, while the Federalists charged that Republican efforts to limit power were aimed at destabilizing all authority.

The whiskey tax spurred frontier protests reminiscent of the 1760s. Farmers in western Pennsylvania, Kentucky, and North Carolina, who turned their corn into whiskey so it could be more easily shipped and sold, raised liberty poles and argued that the excise tax unfairly burdened their cash-poor region with a tax they could not pay. Not content with tarring and feathering the tax collectors, some radicals threatened to burn Pittsburgh.

Frontier farmers argued that the government demanded their support but did nothing for them. The Washington administration had difficulty protecting citizens on the frontier, vulnerable to attacks by Indians supported by the British. General Arthur St. Clair had been sent in November 1791 to pacify the Miami Indians of Ohio; the Miamis and their allies overwhelmed St. Clair's forces, killing or wounding nine hundred of his fourteen hundred men. Meanwhile, Spanish control of the Mississippi blocked the farmers of Pennsylvania, Ohio, western Virginia, and Kentucky from access to the sea.

When western Pennsylvania protestors threatened to overwhelm the local government, President Washington in 1794 sent more than ten thousand troops to put down the Whiskey Rebellion. Frontiersmen pointed out that the government sent ten times as many soldiers to fight them as it had sent to protect them from the Miamis, and that the rebellion had died down by the time the federal army arrived. But that same summer, an army under Anthony Wayne fought the Miami at Fallen Timbers (now Maumee, Ohio). It was a victory, though not decisive, for the Americans; the Shawnee retreated to the British post at Fort Miami but were turned away. The following year the Shawnee and Miami agreed to move out of southern Ohio.

Washington demonstrated the ability of American authorities to secure the frontier from both Indians and frontiersmen. In his annual message to Congress in the wake of the turmoil, Washington congratulated the American people for living under a government that could keep them both safe and free. But he blamed "certain self-created societies"—the Democratic-Republicans—for stirring up political trouble on the frontier and hindering the government's ability to govern. As in the 1760s, two different ideas of government were emerging—Washington's, that the elected government should do its job without interference from the governed; and the opposition's, that the governed have a fundamental right—and a power—to govern their governors. The tension this time would not overthrow the system but would be resolved within it.

When John Adams became president in 1797, the nation's chief problem was with France, which had gone to war against England. The Washington administration declared the United States neutral, but sent Chief Justice John Jay to negotiate a new commercial treaty with England. Feeling betrayed, the French turned their warships against American merchant vessels.

Knowing Vice President Jefferson's popularity in France and his diplomatic skill, Adams thought of sending him to negotiate in Paris. But Jefferson thought it improper for the vice president to negotiate a treaty, and the Federalists opposed sending him. Adams sent a delegation—Marshall, Pinckney, and Gerry—though French bureaucrats refused to talk unless the Americans bribed them. When this news reached Philadelphia, Congress established a navy to protect American commerce, authorized Adams to raise an army (which Washington came out of retirement to command), and passed the Alien and Sedition acts.

Aimed at the Republican press, the sedition law made it a federal offense to write, publish, or utter anything that might bring the president or Congress into contempt, hatred, or ridicule. Fourteen newspaper editors and one Congressman were jailed for sedition. The Alien Friends Act was aimed at Irish immigrants, many of whom were active Republicans—it allowed the deportation of aliens from countries friendly to the United States, who were deemed threats to American peace and safety. The Alien Enemies Act allowed the president to deport any alien, dangerous or not, who came from a country at war with the United States. The Naturalization Act made it more difficult for immigrants to become citizens.

The Sedition Act would expire in March of 1801, meaning there would be two congressional elections and one presidential election while it was against the law to criticize congressmen or the president. Jefferson called it "the reign of the witches," and he and Madison secretly drafted resolutions that the Virginia and Kentucky legislatures adopted, calling the Alien and Sedition laws unconstitutional extensions of federal power. No other states joined in opposition. It seemed the Federalists would secure power using the apparatus of the elected government.

Two things prevented this. One was that a new French government sincerely wanted to negotiate with the Americans; another was that Republicans mobilized for the election of 1800. As Massachusetts Federalist Fisher Ames complained, the Republicans turned every husking bee, every barn raising, and every funeral into a political rally, which swept the Federalists from control of the House, the Senate, and the executive branch. No man alive at the time had ever experienced this—a government in office being replaced by another through a popular election. The ousted government went home.

Thomas Jefferson referred to his election in 1800 as a "revolution," not in the sense of overturning a government, but in the sense of revolving and returning to earlier principles. In his first weeks in office, Jefferson wrote to colleagues who had secured the Revolution of 1776. To John Dickinson he wrote that his administration would "put our ship of state on her republican tack, so she would show by the grace of her movements the skill of her builders." He did not write to John Adams, who left Washington before Jefferson took the oath, but he wrote to Samuel Adams that his inaugural address was a letter to that "patriarch," and he wondered with every line "if this is the spirit" of Samuel Adams.

In his inaugural address Jefferson reflected on the "contest of opinion" through which the nation had just passed, saying the intensity of public discussions might alarm "strangers unused to saying what they think." But now that the matter was decided in accordance with the Constitution, all would peacefully go about their business. As for the political divisions of the 1790s, he noted that "every difference of opinion is not a difference of principle. We have called by different names brethren of the same principles. We are all republicans, we are all federalists."

Would Jefferson use the government's power to punish his political opponents, who had tried to silence the opposition? He would not. The Federalists had mistaken the nature of American power. The government did not need an army to keep domestic peace, or laws to punish dissenting opinions. Its strength rested on an informed citizenry. Without a sedition act or a standing army, this government, which he called "the world's best hope," was the "only one where every man, at the call of the law, will fly to the standard of the law, and will meet violations of the public order as his own personal concern." This was a new idea in the world—that the public order was the personal concern of every citizen.

Jefferson knew that some Federalists feared human nature and doubted the ability of people to govern themselves. "Sometimes it is said that man cannot be trusted with the government of himself." But then he asked, "Can he then be trusted with the government of others? Or have we found angels, in the form of kings, to govern him? Let history answer this question."

Jefferson briefly set out the principles that would shape his administration. The government should prevent men from injuring one another, but otherwise leave them free to regulate their own affairs. If any men wanted to dissolve the union, as the Federalists had accused the Republicans, or alter its republican nature, as the Republicans had charged the Federalists, "let them stand undisturbed as monuments to the freedom with which error of opinion may be tolerated where reason is left free to combat it." These principles, which Jefferson said had guided the nation through an age of revolution and reformation, would remain the fundamental principles of American government at least until the Civil War. Limited government resting on informed opinion was the touchstone of Jefferson's political faith and the faith of the American Revolution.

James Monroe, the last Revolutionary War veteran to serve as president, in 1824 invited Lafayette, the war's last surviving major general, to return to America as the nation's guest. Lafayette had lost his fortune during the French Revolution; his wife had nearly gone to the guillotine, and he had been imprisoned in Austria. Refusing to serve a nonelected government, Lafayette had a cool relationship with France's restored monarchy, which suppressed public demonstrations to bid him farewell. Saying the moment he again set foot on "the shores of freedom" would be "the most delightful I shall ever enjoy," Lafayette—as he had in 1777—slipped out of France, this time accompanied only by his son, his secretary, and his valet.

America had changed since Lafayette's first visit in 1777. So had Europe. In 1777 monarchies dominated the world, and the British, French, Spanish, Portuguese, and Dutch claimed all the Americas. By 1824, the people of Haiti, Argentina, Venezuela, Mexico, Peru, and Brazil, as well as the United States, were independent. Their revolutions had shaken Europe itself. There had been fewer than three million Americans—white and black, not counting Native Americans—all living along the Atlantic coast, when Lafayette first arrived in 1777; now there were twelve million (not counting Indians), and their territory stretched across the continent to the Pacific. They were digging canals across their land and building steamboats to ship their goods across the Atlantic. The American navy patrolled the continent's coasts—Atlantic, Gulf, and Pacific—and President Monroe announced that the United States would not tolerate any European intrusion in the new world. At a Paris celebration of Washington's birthday, Lafayette toasted Monroe's doctrine as another part of "the great contest between the rights of mankind and the pretensions of European despotism and aristocracy."

Lafayette visited all twenty-four states, and it seemed all twelve million Americans turned out to meet him. He remembered the names of veterans who had served with him, he stayed with presidents and political leaders, with free black families and Native Americans, with frontier farmers and city merchants. He laid the cornerstone for the Bunker Hill Monument and brought dirt from the battlefield home so that when he died he could be buried in it.

While Lafayette was unabashed in his enthusiasm for the common cause of liberty, he saw its limits even in America. He had urged Washington to take a stand against slavery even during the Revolution. Washington's thoughts on slavery had changed during the war: on his arrival at Cambridge he had tried to bar black men from serving in the Continental Army. But he had rescinded this order at the end of 1775, and before the war ended he would vow never to buy or sell another human being (a vow he did not keep). By the war's end he also encouraged Henry Laurens, son of a South Carolina planter, in his attempt to raise a regiment of black troops from the enslaved people of South Carolina, who would be given their freedom in return for fighting for the freedom of their owners.

In the 1780s it might have seemed that slavery was being limited. Black men and women in Massachusetts had petitioned in the early 1770s for their liberty. When the new state constitution in 1780 stated that all men were free and equal, slaves in Massachusetts went to court. In the cases of Quock Walker, a slave in Worcester County, and Elizabeth Freeman, a slave in Berkshire County, juries found that under this constitution one person could not own another. By the time of the first census in 1790, Massachusetts was the only state without slaves.

Lafayette visited every state on his triumphal return in 1824–25; in June 1825 he laid the cornerstone of the Bunker Hill Monument; he returned to France with dirt from Bunker Hill which, after his death in 1834, was spread over his grave. (Image courtesy of the Massachusetts Historical Society.)

The Pennsylvania assembly passed a gradual emancipation law in 1780, freeing children born into slavery when they reached the age of twenty-eight. The leaders of Pennsylvania had humanitarian reasons for opposing slavery as well as practical ones. First, it was apparent that the British occupation had been aided by Philadelphia's enslaved people, who hoped for a British victory, which would bring emancipation. Many slaves had left with their Loyalist owners; others went over to the British side. After the occupation, as Philadelphia's economy recovered, skilled white workers sought the positions held by skilled slaves. During and after the war, a move to emancipate slaves coincided with a decline in the black population of the northern states.

In addition to lobbying Washington to take a stand, Lafayette had also urged Jefferson and Madison to make public their private views of slavery. Jefferson's *Notes on the State of Virginia* (1782) had called slavery "the most unremitting despotism," permitting "one half the citizens to trample on the rights of the other," transforming the first into despots, the others into enemies. "Indeed I tremble for my country when I reflect that God is just: that his justice cannot sleep forever," and that "the Almighty has no attribute which can take side with us in such a contest."

But he would say no more. Virginia considered but rejected a gradual emancipation bill in the 1790s; it would not revive the subject again until 1831, after Nat Turner's insurrection in Southampton County. Virginians had supported the 1787 Northwest Ordinance, banning slavery in the territory north of the Ohio River, and President Jefferson urged Congress in 1807 to make good on its constitutional power to end the slave trade. But neither he nor Madison would publicly attack slavery, nor would either free his slaves, as their private secretary Edward Coles had done in 1819, settling the freed people on land he purchased in Illinois. As governor in the 1820s, Coles blocked an attempt to allow slavery into Illinois.

Despite not taking action, Jefferson and Madison, and even Lafayette, might have believed that by barring slavery north of the Ohio and prohibiting the international slave trade they had put slavery on the road to extinction. But by the 1820s the institution was spreading. Slavery had exhausted Virginia's soil, and the Carolina rice plantations had reached their own saturation point. Eli Whitney, a clever Yankee, visited in the 1790s the plantation a grateful Georgia had given Nathanael Greene. Learning of a competition to develop a faster way to clean and card cotton, he entered and won with his "cotton engine," or "gin," which performed the tedious work of cleaning seeds from cotton boles and straightening the fibers. Cotton became the leading American export, grown by slave labor in a fertile belt stretching from Georgia to the west, shipped either to the manufacturing centers of England or to the newly built textile mills of New England. Henry Adams, great-grandson of John, wrote that after 1815 Americans thought more about the price of cotton than about the rights of man; by 1860 a South Carolina senator proclaimed that "Cotton is King."

Cotton's expansion increased the demand for slaves and the values of land in Georgia, Alabama, and Mississippi. In the immediate aftermath of the Revolution, settlers had moved into upstate New York, Ohio, and Kentucky; by the 1820s the boom area was between Georgia and the Mississippi. The impediment to settlement here had been the Choctaws, Creeks, Chickasaws, and Cherokees. Living in large towns and practicing settled agriculture, these "Civilized Tribes" had made treaties with the United States, but the states of Georgia, Alabama, and Mississippi were determined to push them beyond the Mississippi River and open their territory for sale and development as cotton plantations. In 1830 Congress passed the Indian Removal Act, calling for treaties to move all these nations—American allies or enemies—into what became Oklahoma.

This plan had been in place long before. Lafayette was called away from a formal ball held in his honor in Kaskaskia, Illinois, to meet with an Indian woman named Mary. She had come to Illinois in 1800, leaving her shattered Iroquois homeland and the steady white encroachment westward. Her father, the Iroquois warrior Panisciowa, had given her a small leather pouch which held "the most powerful Manitou" to be used with the encroaching whites; all who saw it had shown him marked affection. She brought this talisman to show Lafayette. Inside the pouch Lafayette saw a letter of recommendation he had written for Panisciowa in 1778, now preserved by his daughter as a sacred relic of her father's service in "the good American cause."

Lafayette arrived in Buffalo, which had come into being when Panisciowa and other Iroquois moved west, and then traveled down the new Erie Canal, which connected the great interior to New York and the east coast. The canal towns were springing up out of the forest, with the sounds of saws and hammers constantly in the air as trees fell and buildings rose on their site—first an inn for travelers and newcomers, then schools, printing shops to publish newspapers, and homes. Americans were transforming this world.

At Buffalo Lafayette met an old warrior, Red Jacket. They had met forty years earlier when the Americans and Iroquois made peace at Fort Schuyler. Lafayette asked what became of the "Young Indian who had opposed the burying of the tomahawk with such eloquence?"

"He is standing in front of you," Red Jacket replied.

"Time has changed us much," Lafayette replied. "We were young and agile then." Both were now old men in a young country transforming itself, for good or ill, thanks to the war they had fought half a century earlier.

Back in the capital, Lafayette met an envoy sent by Simon Bolivar, the liberator of Colombia, Venezuela, Ecuador, Bolivia, and Panama, and presented him with a gold medal, a portrait of Washington, and the "personal congratulations of a veteran of the common cause." President John Quincy Adams hosted a White House dinner on September 6, Lafayette's birthday, toasting February 22, the birthday of Washington. Lafayette toasted July 4, the "birthday of liberty in the two hemispheres."

Lafayette stirred American plans to celebrate the fiftieth anniversary of that birthday on July 4, 1826. The Declaration of Independence's three surviving signers—John Adams, Thomas Jefferson, and Charles Carroll of Carrollton, Maryland, were too infirm to attend. Adams and Jefferson would both die on July 4; but all sent messages looking forward to the world their countrymen would continue to create anew.

Jefferson hoped July 4 would "be to the world…the signal of arousing men to burst the chains under which monkish ignorance and superstition had persuaded them to bind themselves, and to assume the blessings and security of self-government," which must be based on the "free right" of unbounded reason. "All eyes are opened, or opening, to the rights of man. The general spread of the light of science has already laid open to every view the palpable truth, that the mass of mankind has not been born with saddles on their backs, nor a favored few booted and spurred, ready to ride them legitimately, by the grace of God. These are grounds of hope for others."

Citizens in Quincy, Massachusetts, asked John Adams to attend their own celebrations on July 4. He declined, but offered a toast. It would be his last public statement. He gave them two words: "Independence forever!"

Would he add more?

"Not a word."

FURTHER READING

Has the history of the Revolution been, as Adams predicted, one continuous lie? Historians have given it more depth and detail than the story Adams expected, that Franklin smote the earth and brought forth Washington. The Revolution spawned an interest in history at the very beginning—the Massachusetts Historical Society (http://www.masshist.org/) was formed in 1791 to preserve documents and materials related to the Revolution; it now houses all the papers of John and Abigail Adams, as well as many papers of Thomas Jefferson, Benjamin Lincoln, and other figures, many of which have now been digitized and are available on the Internet; Isaiah Thomas, printer of the *Massachusetts Spy*, founded in 1812 the American Antiquarian Society in Worcester, which houses collections of newspapers, books, and manuscripts; the Historical Society of Pennsylvania began its collections in 1824; the Virginia Historical Society began in 1831, with John Marshall as its first president and James Madison its first honorary member.

The books listed below will help navigate the Revolution in all its intriguing complexity. Virtually every figure mentioned in this book has been the subject of scholarly research, and the papers of many—Adams, Washington, Franklin, Jefferson, Hamilton, Madison—have been published in annotated editions.

COMPREHENSIVE STUDIES OF THE REVOLUTION AS A WHOLE

Countryman, Edward. *The American Revolution.* New York: Hill and Wang, 1985.

Jensen, Merrill. *The Founding of a Nation: A History of the American Revolution, 1763–1776.* New York: Oxford University Press, 1968.

Middlekauff, Robert. *The Glorious Cause: The American Revolution, 1763–1789.* New York: Oxford University Press, 1982.

Nash, Gary B. *The Unknown American Revolution: The Unruly Birth of Democracy and the Struggle to Create America.* New York: Viking, 2005.

Trevelyan, George Otto. *The American Revolution.* 4 vols. New York: Longmans, Green, 1920–22.

————. *George III and Charles Fox: The Concluding Part of the American Revolution.* 2 vols. New York: Longmans, Green, 1912–15.

Wood, Gordon S. *American Revolution: A History.* New York: Modern Library, 2002.

CONTEMPORARY ACCOUNTS

Gordon, William. *The History of the Rise, Progress, And Establishment, of the Independence of the United States of America: Including an Account of the Late War; and of the Thirteen Colonies, from their Origin to That Period.* London: 1788.

Marshall, John. *The Life of George Washington: Commander in Chief of the American Forces, During the War Which Established the Independence of His Country, and First President of the United States.* Philadelphia: Wayne, 1804–7.

Oliver, Peter. *Origin and Progress of the American Rebellion: A Tory View.* Edited by Douglass Adair and John A. Schutz. San Marino, CA: Huntington Library, 1961.

Ramsay, David. *History of the American Revolution.* Edited by Lester H. Cohen. Indianapolis, IN: Liberty Classics, 1990.

Warren, Mercy Otis. *History of the Rise, Progress, and Termination of the American Revolution: Interspersed with Biographical, Political, and Moral Observations.* Edited by Lester H. Cohen. Indianapolis, IN: Liberty Classics, 1988.

ESSAY COLLECTIONS

Bailyn, Bernard. *Faces of Revolution: Personalities and Themes in the Struggle for American Independence.* New York: Knopf, 1990.

————. *To Begin the World Anew: The Genius and Ambiguities of the American Founders.* New York: Knopf, 2003.

Greene, Jack P. *Understanding the American Revolution: Issues and Actors.* Charlottesville: University of Virginia Press, 1995.

Maier, Pauline. *The Old Revolutionaries: Political Lives in the Age of Samuel Adams.* New York: Knopf, 1980.

MILITARY HISTORY

Higginbotham, Don. *The War of American Independence: Military Attitudes, Policies, and Practice, 1763–1789.* Boston: Northeastern University Press, 1983.

Royster, Charles. *A Revolutionary People at War: The Continental Army and American Character, 1775–1783.* Chapel Hill: University of North Carolina Press, 1979.

Shy, John. *A People Numerous and Armed: Reflections on the Military Struggle for American Independence.* New York: Oxford University Press, 1976.

STUDIES ON THEMES OR EVENTS

Archer, Richard. *As If an Enemy's Country: The British Occupation of Boston and the Origins of Revolution.* New York: Oxford University Press, 2010.

Bailyn, Bernard. *The Ideological Origins of the American Revolution*. Cambridge, MA: Belknap Press of Harvard University Press, 1967.

————. *The Ordeal of Thomas Hutchinson*. Cambridge, MA: Belknap Press of Harvard University Press, 1974.

Berkin, Carol. *Revolutionary Mothers: Women in the Struggle for America's Independence*. New York: Knopf, 2005.

Buel, Joy Day, and Richard Buel Jr. *The Way of Duty: A Woman and Her Family in Revolutionary America*. New York: Norton, 1984.

Calloway, Colin G. *The American Revolution in Indian Country: Crisis and Diversity in Native American Communities*. Cambridge: Cambridge University Press, 1995.

Egerton, Douglas R. *Death or Liberty: African Americans and Revolutionary America*. New York: Oxford University Press, 2009.

Ellis, Joseph J. *American Creation: Triumphs and Tragedies at the Founding of the Republic*. New York: Knopf, 2007.

————. *Founding Brothers: The Revolutionary Generation*. New York: Knopf, 2000.

Fischer, David Hackett. *Paul Revere's Ride*. New York: Oxford University Press, 1994.

————. *Washington's Crossing*. New York: Oxford University Press, 2004.

Fowler, William M., Jr. *Empires at War: The French and Indian War and the Struggle for North America, 1754–1763*. New York: Walker, 2005.

————. *Rebels Under Sail: The American Navy during the Revolution*. New York: Scribner, 1976.

Glatthaar, Joseph, and James Kirby Martin, *Forgotten Allies: The Oneida Indians and the American Revolution*. New York: Hill and Wang, 2006.

Gould, Eliga H. *The Persistence of Empire: British Political Culture in the Age of the American Revolution*. Chapel Hill: University of North Carolina Press, 2000.

Gross, Robert A. *The Minutemen and Their World*. New York: Hill and Wang, 1976.

Higginbotham, Don. *Revolution in America: Considerations and Comparisons*. Charlottesville: University of Virginia Press, 2005.

Hoffman, Ronald, and Peter J. Albert, eds. *Arms and Independence: The Military Character of the American Revolution*. Charlottesville: University of Virginia Press, 1984.

Kerber, Linda K. *Women of the Republic: Intellect and Ideology in Revolutionary America*. Chapel Hill: University of North Carolina Press, 1980.

MacLeod, Duncan J. *Slavery, Race, and the American Revolution*. London: Cambridge University Press, 1974.

Maier, Pauline. *American Scripture: Making the Declaration of Independence*. New York: Knopf, 1997.

————. *From Resistance to Revolution: Colonial Radicals and the Development of American Opposition to Britain, 1765–1776*. New York: Knopf, 1972.

McDonnell, Michael A. *The Politics of War: Race, Class, and Conflict in Revolutionary Virginia*. Chapel Hill: University of North Carolina Press, 2007.

98 • FURTHER READING

Morgan, Edmund S., and Helen M. Morgan. *The Stamp Act Crisis: Prologue to Revolution*. Chapel Hill: University of North Carolina Press, 1953.

Nash, Gary B. *The Forgotten Fifth: African Americans in the Age of Revolution*. Cambridge, MA: Harvard University Press, 2006.

———. *Race and Revolution*. Madison, WI: Madison House, 1990.

———. *The Urban Crucible: Social Change, Political Consciousness, and the Origins of the American Revolution*. Cambridge, MA: Harvard University Press, 1979.

Nevins, Allan. *The American States During and After the Revolution, 1775–1789*. New York: Macmillan, 1924.

Norton, Mary Beth. *The British-Americans: Loyalist Exiles in England, 1774–1789*. Boston: Little, Brown, 1972.

———. *Liberty's Daughters: The Revolutionary Experience of American Women, 1750–1800*. Ithaca, NY: Cornell University Press, 1996.

Ragosta, John A. *Wellspring of Liberty: How Virginia's Religious Dissenters Helped Win the American Revolution and Secured Religious Liberty*. New York: Oxford University Press, 2010.

Slaughter, Thomas P. *The Whiskey Rebellion: Frontier Epilogue to the American Revolution*. New York: Oxford University Press, 1986.

Sosin, Jack M. *The Revolutionary Frontier, 1763–1783*. New York: Holt, Rinehart and Winston, 1967.

Wood, Gordon S. *The Creation of the American Republic, 1776–1787*. Chapel Hill: University of North Carolina Press, 1969.

Young, Alfred F. *Masquerade: The Life and Times of Deborah Sampson, Continental Soldier*. New York: Knopf, 2004.

———. *The Shoemaker and the Tea Party: Memory and the American Revolution*. Boston: Beacon, 1999.

BIOGRAPHIES

Black, Jeremy. *George III: America's Last King*. New Haven, CT: Yale University Press, 2006.

Ellis, Joseph J. *His Excellency, George Washington*. New York: Knopf, 2004.

———. *Passionate Sage: The Character and Legacy of John Adams*. New York: Norton, 1993.

Foner, Eric. *Tom Paine and Revolutionary America*. Rev. ed. New York: Oxford University Press, 2004.

Fowler, William M., Jr. *The Baron of Beacon Hill: A Biography of John Hancock*. Boston: Houghton Mifflin, 1979.

———. *Samuel Adams: Radical Puritan*. New York: Longman, 1997.

Freeman, Douglas Southall. *George Washington: A Biography*. 7 vols. New York: Scribner, 1948–57.

Greene, George Washington. *The Life of Nathanael Greene, Major-General in the Army of the Revolution*. 3 vols. New York: Hurd & Houghton, 1871.

Gruber, Ira D. *The Howe Brothers and the American Revolution*. New York: Atheneum, 1972.

Martin, James Kirby. *Benedict Arnold, Revolutionary Hero: An American Warrior Reconsidered*. New York: New York University Press, 1997.

Mayer, Henry. *A Son of Thunder: Patrick Henry and the American Republic*. New York: Watts, 1986.

McCoy, Drew R. *Last of the Fathers: James Madison and the Republican Legacy*. Cambridge: Cambridge University Press, 1989.

McCullough, David. *John Adams*. New York: Simon & Schuster, 2001.

Miller, Marla R. *Betsy Ross and the Making of America*. New York: Henry Holt, 2010.

Peterson, Merrill D. *Thomas Jefferson and the New Nation: A Biography*. New York: Oxford University Press, 1970.

Puls, Mark. *Henry Knox: Visionary General of the American Revolution*. New York: Palgrave Macmillan, 2008.

Van Doren, Carl. *Benjamin Franklin*. New York: Viking, 1938.

Willcox, William B. *Portrait of a General: Sir Henry Clinton in the War of Independence*. New York: Knopf, 1964.

INDEX

Dunlap, John, 35
Dunmore, John M. (Lord), 13–14, 25

East India Company, 16
Eden, William, 50
electoral vote, 80
Ellsworth, Oliver, 78, 81
emancipation: gradual, 91, 92;
    Massachusetts petition for, 90
England: French declaration of war
    on, *45*; Spain at war with, 56; war
    dilemma for, 49–50
Episcopal clergy, Virginia's, 75
d'Estaing (comte d'), 54–55

Fallen Timbers, 86
federal government, 76–84
Federalists, 82, 83, 85–86, 89
Fort Lee, 38–39
Fort Miami, 86
Fort Ticonderoga, 27, 38
Fort Washington, 38
France, 93; British empire threatened
    by, 1, 4, 15; U.S. independence
    acknowledged by, 49; war against
    England, *45*; war support by, 44–47,
    60–61; West Indies territories of, 66
Franklin, Benjamin, xvii, 27; on British
    Empire, 3–4; "common origins"
    of, 77; Paris reception, 44; in peace
    talks, 22; Stamp Act protest explained
    by, 8–9; Staten Island meeting
    with, 37; voting rights speech of, 79
freeholders, voting rights restricted
    to, 78–79
French officers: under Rochambeau,
    60–61, *67*; in Washington's
    deploy, 60–61
French revolution, 84–85, 86

Gage, Thomas, 17–18, 19, 22, 23
Galloway, Joseph, 50
Gates, Horatio, 71
George III, 8, 16, 29, 46; charges
    against, 32–33, *34*;
    destruction of statue of, 35
Georgia: British occupation of, 58;
    British retaking of, 56; Clinton's
    South Carolina strategy and, 65;
    Constitution ratified by, 83; founding
    of colonial, 3
Germain, George, 28, 48

Germans, 48, 50
Gerry, Elbridge, 77, 81
government, 19, 30, 50; colonial self-, 2;
    confederation v. people and, 76.
    See also federal government
gradual emancipation, 91, 92
de Grasse. *See* Paul, François-Joseph
Greene, Nathanael, 24, 46, 50
Green Mountain Boys, 21
guerilla warfare, in Carolinas, 59

habeas corpus, 82
Hamilton, Alexander, 53, 77, 84, 85–86
Hancock, John, 23, 77, 83
hanging, Andre's, 63
Hays, William, *54*
Hector, Charles (count d'Estaing), 54–55
Henry, Patrick, 7, 77, 83–84
Hessians, 40, 41, 53
Hopkins, Stephen, 15
Horrid Massacre, Boston, 11–13, *12*, 33
House of Representatives, 80, 84
Howe, Catherine, 36
Howe, Richard, 35, 36
Howe, William, 22–25, 27, 28, 51;
    Adams, J., at Staten Island with, 37;
    attack on Washington, 37–40; goal/
    means of Washington v., *43*;
    meschianza in honor of, 51–53, *52*; in
    New York, 55; in Philadelphia, 48;
    war strategies of, 49
Hudson River, 69
human nature, Jefferson on trust in, 89
Hutchinson, Thomas, 4–5, 12

immigrants, South Carolina slaves as, 3
imperialism, New England colonial, 2
independence: beginnings of, 30–43;
    complexities of, 31; declaration
    of, 31–35, *34*, 94; Louis XVI
    recognizing U.S., 49; Washington's
    view of union and, 73
Indian Removal Act, 93
Indians. *See* Native Americans
Intolerable Acts, 18
Iroquois, 2, 4, *47*, 57

Jamaica, 1, 2
James, Henry, 39
Jay, John, 84
Jefferson, Thomas, 32, 84; Declaration
    of Independence and, 94; on human

Samson, Deborah, 70
Savannah, 58
Scott, William, 69
sea raids, 56–57
secretary of treasury, first, 84
Sedition Act, 87–88
settlement, Native American impediment
   to, 92
Shawnees, 14, 58, 86
Sherman, Roger, 77
Shurtliff, Robert, 70
Shy, John, 69
Skinners, 60
slavery, 3, 6, 90; British occupation
   aided by, 91; Constitution and, 84;
   declaration of independence on, 33;
   Jefferson on, 91–92; voting rights
   and, 78–79; Washington's changed
   view of, 90
slave trade, 80–81
smuggling, 15
soldier, woman disguised as male, 70
Sons of Liberty, 7, 11, 14, 17
South Carolina, 30, 55, 63, 65;
   black majority in, 30;
   British occupation of, 58;
   Clinton's strategy for Georgia and, 65;
   Cornwallis retreat to, 63, 65;
   cotton plantations in, 92;
   delegates from, 77;
   ratification by, 83
Spain, 56, 66
spinning wheels, 11
Stamp Act, 7–10, 9, 68, 75
Staten Island conference, 37
states: 1780s slavery in, 90; churches
   in, 74; constitutions, 78–79; power
   of, 76; ratification of Constitution,
   83–84; taxation/power and, 77–78
Steuben, Friedrich Wilhelm von, 50–51
Stewart, Walter, 71
Sugar Act, 5–6
sugar economy, 1, 25
Sullivan, John, 46, 55, 57
Sumter, Thomas, 59

tariff, slave, 81
Tarleton, Banastre, 59, 65
taxation: colonial opposition to, 6–13, 9;
   principle of representation with, 74–75;
   Stamp Act, 7–10, 9, 68, 75; state
   powers of, 77–78; tea, 13, 16–26, 32,

75; Virginia Baptists, 74–76, 84;
   whiskey, 86
Tea Act, 16–26, 32, 75
territory: disputes over, 2; French West
   Indies, 66; Native American-frontiers-
   men, 86–87; Parliament extension of
   Quebec, 18
Thomas, John, 27
Ticonderoga, 27, 38
tobacco, 2
Townshend, Charles, 7, 10–11
Townshend Acts, 11
trade, 2, 3, 4, 6; slave, 80–81
Trenton, Washington's victory at, 41–43
troops. See British troops; rebel troops;
   Russian troops, efforts to recruit
two-house legislature, 77–78
tyranny, majority, 76

United States (U.S.): first appearance in
   print, 35; French recognition of
   independent, 49; new name, 35.
   See also presidents

Valley Forge, 50, 54
vice president, Adams, J., as, 84
Vincennes, 57
A Vindication of the Rights of Man
   (Paine), 85
Virginia, 92; constitution of, 78–79;
   delegates, 76–77; legal code of, 75;
   Madison–Henry faceoff in, 83–84;
   taxation of Baptists in, 74–76, 84; war
   strategies in, 65–66
voting, 78–79, 80, 81

Walker, Quock, 90
Walpole, Horace, 15, 47
war: civil, 81–82, 89; France-
   England, 45; against Native
   Americans, 13–14; Spain-
   England, 56; war of
   independence. See Revolution
warships, 15, 17, 56, 61, 62
Washington, George, xvii, 3, 5, 36, 43,
   60; Alleghany/Monongahela war
   started by, 5; Congressional Medal of
   Honor given, 28; Cornwallis
   surrender and, 68; as first
   president, 84–87; French officers
   deployed by, 60–61; Howe, W., attack
   on, 37–40; independence viewed